Twelve More Modern Scottish Poets

edited by
Charles King
and Iain Crichton Smith

Hodder and Stoughton

London   Sydney   Auckland   Toronto

The publisher acknowledges subsidy from
the Scottish Arts Council towards the
publication of this volume

First published 1986

British Library Cataloguing in Publication Data

King, Charles, *1919–*
    Twelve more modern Scottish poets.
    1. English poetry — Scottish authors
    2. Scottish poetry — 20th century
    I. Title   II. Crichton Smith, Iain
    821'.914'0809411 PR8658

    ISBN 0 340 39072 7 (PBK)
    ISBN 0 340 40363 2 (BDS)

Printed in Great Britain for
Hodder and Stoughton Educational,
a division of Hodder and Stoughton Ltd,
Mill Road, Dunton Green, Sevenoaks, Kent,
by Holmes McDougall Ltd., Edinburgh

Contents

Maurice Lindsay (b. 1918)

W. S. Graham (1918–86)

Derick Thomson (b. 1921)

Alastair Mackie (b. 1925)

Burns Singer (1928–64)

Stewart Conn (b. 1936)

Douglas Dunn (b. 1942)

Tom Leonard (b. 1944)

Liz Lochhead (b. 1948)

Valerie Gillies (b. 1948)

Acknowledgments

The editors and publishers thank the following for permission to reproduce copyright material: Mrs Paddy Fraser for the poems of George Sutherland Fraser; W. L. Memorial Trust Fund for the poems of George Campbell Hay © George Campbell Hay (Deorsa Mac Iain Deorsa), 1947, 1948, 1952; Mrs Nessie Graham for the poems of W. S. Graham; Maurice Lindsay for his poems; Derick Thomson for his poems; Alastair Mackie for his poems; Carcanet Press Ltd for the poems of Burns Singer; Stewart Conn for his poems; poems by Douglas Dunn from *Terry Street*, *The Happier Life*, *Love or Nothing*, *Barbarians*, *St Kilda's Parliament* and *Elegies* reprinted by permission of Faber and Faber Ltd; Tom Leonard for his poems; Liz Lochhead for her poems © Liz Lochhead, first published in *Dreaming Frankenstein and other poems*, published by Polygon Books; and Valerie Gillies for her poems.

The editors and publishers also wish to thank the following for permission to use photos: The Scottish Tourist Board (for the cover photo), the Trustees of the National Library of Scotland (for the photos of George Campbell Hay and Burns Singer), Sally Fear, Camera Press (for the photo of W. S. Graham), John Watt (for the photo of Maurice Lindsay), *Radio Times* (for the photo of Stewart Conn), Michael Leonard (for the photo of Tom Leonard), Scotsman Publications Ltd (for the photo of Liz Lochhead) and Yerbury (for the photo of Valerie Gillies).

To Hugh MacDiarmid and Sorley Maclean
for opening doors

Introduction

As a result of the continuing success of *Twelve Modern Scottish Poets* (edited by Charles King and published in 1971) it seemed to us that the time was ripe for a second anthology of twelve (different) modern Scottish poets. It contains selections from younger poets who might be said to show in their different and individual ways the continuing strength of Scottish poetry, while also including poets not featured in the first anthology, who seemed to us significant writers. There is work by two very important Gaelic writers (Derick Thomson, also known as Ruaraidh MacThomais), and George Campbell Hay. Scots is represented by Alastair Mackie who has emerged as perhaps the most important of the current poets writing in that language, while of course in the Glasgow dialect we have the inimitable Tom Leonard whose poetry is being seen more and more as not only seminal but also widely successful. George Campbell Hay was unusual in that he wrote in Scots as well as in Gaelic and in English. Thus we hope there is linguistic variety in the anthology reflecting the vital language range in Scotland.

Geographically too, the poets represent many areas. Thus from the north-east we have Mackie, Fraser, and to a certain extent Singer, who worked for a while in Aberdeen and one of whose most beautiful poems is about Peterhead; from Ayrshire, Stewart Conn, whose poems about the farm country there are exact and moving, though he writes from a Glasgow environment as well; from the central belt we have Maurice Lindsay, Tom Leonard, Liz Lochhead and, originally from the Greenock area, W. S. Graham, though he lived for many years outside Scotland. However, some of his most vital poems are set in Scotland. Douglas Dunn has also lived outside Scotland for a large part of his life (though he has now moved back there) and in his case too there are plenty of poems with a Scottish resonance and subject matter. From Lewis in the Outer Hebrides we have Derick Thomson; and in Gaelic George Campbell Hay, some of whose best work is set in Argyll. Also included are some very fine poems of George Campbell Hay set in the Middle East. Finally we have Valerie Gillies, now living in Edinburgh, some of whose verse also has an exotic background, in her case India. It can be seen that the central belt is becoming more and more important, reflecting a trend in modern Scottish literature generally. This was not determined by the editors: it arose naturally from the selection. As a matter of fact the only inflexible criterion the editors used was that *both* should admire the work of the poets included.

A lot of hard work went into the selection of these poets who were chosen from a leet which the editors had drawn up, seeking advice in the process. We hope that the selection finally does justice to the individual poets concerned as well as providing an interesting and challenging experience for the reader.

There are one or two differences between the arrangement of this anthology and the previous one. For one thing there is a photograph of each poet: there is also an introductory piece written by each poet about his relation to his art, as well as perhaps its genesis. As in the previous anthology, however, a bibliography has been provided in order that readers might be able the more easily to pursue interest in a particular poet or poets. In the case of the Gaelic poets there are translations, made in most instances by the poets themselves. It should also be mentioned that a number of poems in this anthology are published for the first time, and for these as well as for other poems used we thank the authors.

As in the case of the previous anthology it is intended that upper schools and colleges may benefit from the selection, and therefore accessibility has been an important factor. This for instance governed the editors' selection from Graham and Singer, some of whose poetry can be difficult and demanding.

We could not have compiled this anthology without assistance of various kinds. First of all, we would like to thank the poets themselves (and their executors in one or two instances) for their kind and most willing cooperation. We owe thanks to Grampian English teachers Margaret Eleftheriou, Andrew Macdonald and Celia Craig for their expert advice from the point of view of the teacher; Norman MacCaig and Edwin Morgan kindly gave counsel; and Mrs Maureen Kemp of Grampian Region is owed much gratitude for her patient and expert typing of a large part of the manuscript.

Finally we would like to thank Elisabeth Bolshaw, our editor at Hodder and Stoughton, for her suggestions and most valuable assistance in providing such an attractive volume.

Charles King
Iain Crichton Smith

G. S. Fraser

G. S. Fraser (1915–80) was one of the
outstanding literary critics of this century.
His earlier autobiography *A Stranger and
Afraid* brings out the essential modesty of
this gifted and committed writer, trained
in the classical mould of Pope. Yet there is
more of Goldsmith in his satire than of
Pope for he is essentially kindly both as
critic and commentator on his fellow man.
His schooling was at Aberdeen Grammar
School; his training as a journalist with the
Press & Journal. That period had an indel-
ible influence on his work and life. Some of
his best writing was from this period of
War Service in the Middle East. His full

stature as a poet became clear in 1981 with the posthumous publication
of the (collected) *Poems of G. S. Fraser* by Leicester University Press.

Poetry is my main gift. But to earn a living I became first a literary
journalist, then a university teacher, and now teaching, especially the
teaching of poetry, has become as true a vocation as writing poetry . . .
Like many Scottish poets I am old-fashioned in my taste for strict metrics
and explicit poetic statement.

I think my best poems have been, in a sense, 'occasional' responses to
particular scenes and situations (Egypt in the Second World War) of a
partly reflective, partly descriptive kind. The feelings tend to be subjective
and personal and for that very reason I usually need a strict form and a
clear pattern of statement. Lately I have become much more experi-
mental, particularly in the use of unrhymed syllabic verse. I am very
conscious of the poem as something to be read aloud, though not in an
over-dramatic manner. I worry most about the true modulation of
feeling in verse. I am a rather intermittent writer, never trying to 'force' a
poem. I think my productivity was cut down a great deal in the 1950s and
after, first by reviewing much current verse, later by teaching students to
appreciate great poetry. I have grown more and more fastidious about my

own poems, though not in the least dispirited about the best of them. I have thought of myself as a rather forgotten poet, but have been pleased in recent years to find that many people know some of my poems and that students seem to respond to them.

from *Contemporary Poets*, published by
St James's Press 1975.

George Sutherland Fraser 1915–80. Born in Glasgow, educated at Glasgow Academy, Aberdeen Grammar School and St Andrews University. Served in the Middle East 1939–45. Married Eileen Lucy Andrew in 1946; two daughters and one son. Journalist *Aberdeen Press & Journal* 1937–39. Freelance journalist in London 1946–58. Cultural Adviser to the U.K. Liaison Mission in Japan 1950–51. Regular reviewer and leader writer for the *Times Literary Supplement*, reviewer for the *New Statesman* and 'New Poetry' Broadcaster for B.B.C. radio in the 1950s. Lecturer in English at The University of Leicester 1958–63. Reader in Poetry at Leicester from 1963 to his death in 1980. Visiting Professor at The University of Rochester, New York 1963–64.

Lean Street

Here, where the baby paddles in the gutter,
  Here in the slaty greyness and the gas,
Here where the women wear dark shawls and mutter
  A hasty word as other women pass,

Telling the secret, telling, clucking and tutting,
  Sighing, or saying that it served her right,
The bitch! — the words and weather both are cutting
  In Causewayend, on this November night.

At pavement's end and in the slaty weather
  I stare with glazing eyes at meagre stone,
Rain and the gas are sputtering together
  A dreary tune! O leave my heart alone,

O leave my heart alone, I tell my sorrows,
  For I will soothe you in a softer bed
And I will numb your grief with fat to-morrows
  Who break your milk teeth on this stony bread!

They do not hear. Thought stings me like an adder,
A doorway's sagging plumb-line squints at me,
The fat sky gurgles like a swollen bladder
    With the foul rain that rains on poverty.

Meditation of a Patriot

The posters show my country blonde and green,
Like some sweet siren, but the travellers know
How dull the shale sky is, the airs how keen,
And how our boorish manners freeze like snow.
Romantic Scotland was an emigrant,
Half-blooded, and escaped from sullen weather.
Here, we toss off a dram to drown a cough
And whisky has the trade-mark of the heather.
My heart yearns southwards as the shadows slant,
I wish I were an exile and I rave:
    With Byron and with Lermontov
    Romantic Scotland's in the grave.

In Glasgow, that damned sprawling evil town,
I interview a vulgar editor,
Who, brawny, self-made, looks me up and down
And seems to wonder what my sort is for.
Do I write verse? Ah, man, but that is bad . . .
And, too polite, I fawn upon this tough,
But when I leave him, O my heart is sad.
He sings alone who in this province sings.
I kick a lamp-post, and in drink I rave:
    With Byron and with Lermontov
    Romantic Scotland's in the grave.

In the far islands to the north and west
Mackenzie and MacDiarmid have their peace.
St Andrews soothes that critic at her breast
Whose polished verse ne'er gave his soul release.
I have no islands and no ancient stone,
Only the sugary granite glittering crisp
Pleases the eye, but turns affection off,
Hard rhetoric, that never learned to lisp.

This town has beauty, but I walk alone
And to the flat and sallow sands I rave:
With Byron and with Lermontov
Romantic Scotland's in the grave.

To Hugh MacDiarmid

Since mine was never the heroic gesture,
    Trained to slick city from my childhood's days,
Only a rambling garden's artful leisure
    Giving my mind its privacy and ease,

Since Poverty for me has never sharpened
    Her single tooth, and since Adversity
So far has failed to jab me with her hair-pin
    I marvel who my Scottish Muse can be.

I am Convention's child, the cub reporter,
    The sleek, the smooth, conservatively poised:
Abandoned long ago by Beauty's daughter;
    Tamed like a broncho, and commercialised!

Perhaps I have a heart that feels . . . I wonder!
    At least I can salute your courage high,
Your thought that burns language to a cinder,
    Your anger, and your angry poet's joy.

O warrior, with the world and wind against you,
    Old sea-bird, in your bleak and rocky coign,
Only my fears can follow where you fly to . . .
    Beneath these rocks, how many souls lie slain!

Your journey has not been the private journey
    Through a mad loveliness, of Hölderlin.
Against the windmills, sir, you choose to tourney.
    And yet, by marvellous chance, you hold your own.

O true bright sword! Perhaps, like Mithridates,
    Before the night has fallen, you may say:
Now I am satisfied: at least my hate is:
    Now let me die: I saw the English flee.

Facing boys' faces, whom your world of thunder
  Is massing clouds for, whom the violet forks
Seek out from heaven . . . simulating candour
  I face both ways! A secret question carks.

Because my love was never for the common
  But only for the rare, the singular air,
Or the undifferenced and naked human,
  Your Keltic mythos shudders me with fear.

What a race has is always crude and common,
  And not the human or the personal:
I would take sword up only for the human,
  Not to revive the broken ghosts of Gael.

Sonnet

My simple heart, bred in provincial tenderness,
And my cold mind, that takes the world for theme,
With local pain, with universal remedy,
Avert the real, disturb the noble dream:

And if my hand could touch you timidly,
Or I could laugh with you, and worry less
About the loud guns laughing over Europe,
I might find a local remedy, a province's hope:

Or if I had the hard steel mind of Lenin,
The skill or even the rage of Catiline
Against the corrupt, the comfortable. Then in

The pages of history one page might be mine.
But for my heart my mind must lose its scope,
And for my mind my heart must give up hope.

Home Town Elegy

(For Aberdeen in Spring)

Glitter of mica at the windy corners,
Tar in the nostrils, under blue lamps budding
Like bubbles of glass the blue buds of a tree,
Night-shining shopfronts, or the sleek sun flooding
The broad abundant dying sprawl of the Dee:
For these and for their like my thoughts are mourners
That yet shall stand, though I come home no more,
Gas-works, white ballroom, and the red brick baths
And salmon nets along a mile of shore,
Or beyond the municipal golf-course, the moorland paths
And the country lying quiet and full of farms.
This is the shape of a land that outlasts a strategy
And is not to be taken with rhetoric or arms.
Or my own room, with a dozen books on the bed
(Too late, still musing what I mused, I lie
And read too lovingly what I have read),
Brantome, Spinoza, Yeats, the bawdy and wise,
Continuing their interminable debate,
With no conclusion, they conclude too late,
When their wisdom has fallen like a grey pall on my eyes.
Syne we maun part, their sall be nane remeid —
Unless my country is my pride, indeed,
Or I can make my town that homely fame
That Byron has, from boys in Carden Place,
Struggling home with books to midday dinner,
For whom he is not the romantic sinner,
The careless writer, the tormented face,
The hectoring bully or the noble fool,
But, just like Gordon or like Keith, a name:
A tall, proud statue at the Grammar School.

Christmas Letter Home

(*To my sister in Aberdeen*)

Drifting and innocent and sad like snow,
Now memories tease me, wherever I go,
And I think of the glitter of granite and distances
And against the blue air the lovely and bare trees,
And slippery pavements spangled with delight
Under the needles of a winter's night,
And I remember the dances, with scarf and cane,
Strolling home in the cold with the silly refrain
Of a tune of Cole Porter or Irving Berlin
Warming a naughty memory up like gin,

And Bunny and Sheila and Joyce and Rosemary
Chattering on sofas or preparing tea,
With their delicate voices and their small white hands
This is the sorrow everyone understands.
More than Rostov's artillery, more than the planes
Skirting the cyclonic islands, this remains,
The little, lovely taste of youth we had:
The guns and not our silliness were mad,
All the unloved and ugly seeking power
Were mad, and not our trivial evening hour
Of swirling taffetas and muslin girls,
Oh, not their hands, their profiles, or their curls,
Oh, not the evenings of coffee and sherry and snow,
Oh, not the music. Let us rise and go —
But then the months and oceans lie between,
And once again the dust of spring, the green
Bright beaks of buds upon the poplar trees,
And summer's strawberries, and autumn's ease,
And all the marble gestures of the dead,
Before my eyes caress against your head,
Your tiny strawberry mouth, your bell of hair,
Your blue eyes with their deep and shallow stare,
Before your hand upon my arm can still
The nerves that everything but home makes ill:
In this historic poster-world I move,
Noise, movement, emptiness, but never love.

Yet all this grief we had to have my dear,
And most who grieve have never known, I fear,
The lucky streak for which we die and live,
And to the luckless must the lucky give
All trust, all energy, whatever lies
Under the anger of democracies:
Whatever strikes the towering torturer down,
Whatever can outface the bully's frown,
Talk to the stammerer, spare a cigarette
For tramps at midnight . . . oh, defend it yet!
Some Christmas I shall meet you. Oh, and then
Though all the boys you used to like are men,
Though all my girls are married, though my verse
Has pretty steadily been growing worse,
We shall be happy: we shall smile and say,
'These years! It only seems like yesterday
I saw you sitting in that very chair.'
'You have not changed the way you do your hair.'
'These years were painful, then?' 'I hardly know.
Something lies gently over them, like snow,
A sort of numbing white forgetfulness . . .'

And so, good-night, this Christmas, and God bless!

The Traveller has Regrets

The traveller has regrets
For the receding shore
That with its many nets
Has caught, not to restore,
The white lights in the bay,
The blue lights on the hill,
Though night with many stars
May travel with him still,
But night has nought to say,
Only a colour and shape
Changing like cloth shaking,
A dancer with a cape
Whose dance is heart-breaking;

Night with its many stars
Can warn travellers
There's only time to kill
And nothing much to say:
But the blue lights on the hill,
The white lights in the bay
Told us the meal was laid
And that the bed was made
And that we could not stay.

Egypt

Who knows the lights at last, who knows the cities
And the unloving hands upon the thighs
Would yet return to seek his home-town pretties
For the shy finger-tips and sidelong eyes.

Who knows the world, the flesh, the compromises
Would go back to the theory in the book:
Who knows the place the poster advertises
Back to the poster for another look.

But nets the fellah spreads beside the river
Where the green waters criss-cross in the sun
End certain migratory hopes for ever:
In that white light, all shadows are undone.

The desert slays. But safe from Allah's justice
Where the broad river of His Mercy lies,
Where ground for labour, or where scope for lust is,
The crooked and tall and cunning cities rise.

The green Nile irrigates a barren region,
All the coarse palms are ankle-deep in sand:
No love roots deep, though easy loves are legion:
The heart's as hot and hungry as the hand.

In airless evenings, at the café table,
The soldier sips his thick sweet coffee up:
The dry grounds, like the moral to my fable,
Are bitter at the bottom of the cup.

An Elegy for Keith Bullen

(Headmaster of Gezira Preparatory School, Cairo, and a friend to English poetry and poets)

A great room and a bowl full of roses,
Red roses, a man as round as a ripe rose,
Lying in a bowl of sun. And who supposes
Such a sad weight could support such a gay pose.

Flying his sad weight like a round baby's
Petulant balloon! He has blue pebbles for eyes,
Petulant, bewildered, innocent eyes like a baby's;
Like a great baby or a clipped rose he lies

In a white bowl of light in my memory;
And expands his tenuous sweetness like a balloon;
I shall die of feeling his dear absurdity
So near me now, if I cannot cry soon.

Keith was particularly Sunday morning,
Red roses, old brandy, was unharrying Time,
Was that white light, our youth; or was the fawning
Zephyr that bobs the gay balloon of rhyme,

He bobbed incredibly in our modern air;
With his loose jacket, his white panama hat,
As he leaned on his walking stick on the stone stair
He seemed a balloon, moored down to the ground by that.

As he leaned at the bar and ordered us pink gin
Or arranged a flutter on the three-fifteen
He seemed a child, incapable of sin:
We never knew him prudent, cold, or mean.

Or tied to the way the world works at all
(Not even tied enough for poetry);
All that he was we only may recall,
An innocent that guilt would wish to be,

A kind, a careless, and a generous,
An unselfseeking in his love of art,
A jolly in his great explosive fuss;
O plethora of roses, O great heart!

The Soldier and the Artist

Great Captains spot the truth and tell:
'He drinks, he's dirty, there's a smell . . .
There's *something* wrong about this chap! . . .
Of women. Did he once get clap?'

He was a great wrecked galleon, yes:
The soldier was a safe success.
Their craft collided over Styx.
The Man of War was knocked for six.

Note: From an anecdote of Douglas Cooper's about Field Marshal Montgomery's dislike of Augustus John.

For my Wife on her Fiftieth Birthday

A little time is fifty years
For so much joy,
                    so many tears,

Nor fifty summers were too long
For every summer
                    was a song

That echoed through
                    the winter's cold
And but one tale the burden told:

She shall have labour, pain, and woe,
She shall bring love
                    where'er she go.

Snow, rain and sun of all her hours
Shall shine among her loves
                    like flowers

That are not flowers of a day.
O how they shine
                    and not decay!

So let us gather roses now
To deck a
   matron Muse's brow,

Slim on her stem, herself a rose.

How time stands still now, so time flows!

Catullus: XXII

Varus, you know Suffenus well. He is
Handsome, and quite a wit, and nicely mannered,
And the most copious scribbler in the world.
He must have written quite ten thousand verses,
Or more, and not like other folk on scraps,
But on imperial paper, in new rolls,
New bosses, fine red ribbon, parchment covers,
All ruled with lead, and all smoothed out with pumice.
And when you read these, this smooth pretty fellow
Suddenly seems a goatherd or a navvy:
It's so absurd and such a total change.

What shall we say about this? Here's a man
More than just bright and gay and affable
Who suddenly becomes a hick of hicks
Taking to poetry: yet a man who's never
Really so happy as when writing poems:
That's what he likes and worships in himself.
Well, we all fall this way. There's not a person
Whom in some matter you can fail to see
To be Suffenus. Each has his own pet maggot:
We cannot see what hangs behind our backs.

George Campbell Hay

George Campbell Hay was one of the most important Gaelic poets of this century (though he also wrote in Scots and English, and translated from a bewildering variety of languages). He was the son of J. MacDougall Hay, author of the famous Scottish novel *Gillespie*: and was born in Argyll.

Many of his early poems are about places and natural phenomena, and he shows a tender love of locality. Some too are about Scotland, for he was a fervent Scottish patriot throughout his life.

However, it is probably his poems set in the Middle East which will be his enduring memorial. (Hay served in that area during the Second World War.) The poem 'Atman' for instance contrasts the humanity of the thief with the inhumanity of the judge. The poem 'Bizerta' is about the violence of war, the more eerie because of the silence that surrounds it. It is one of the great war poems of the twentieth century.

More recently an incomplete long poem of his has been discovered, which extends his exploration of the Arab mentality and customs. It is called 'Mochtar and Dugald'. It was difficult to find in this a suitable extract, however, though it is one of his very finest poems.

While acknowledging that he wrote in Scots and English, there is little doubt that it was as a Gaelic poet that he achieved his purest mastery. It is hoped that the translations included here will give an idea of the feminine tenderness of his love of place, as well as his love of humanity and hatred of violence.

George Campbell Hay (1915–84), the son of John MacDougall Hay (1881–1919), author of the novel *Gillespie*, was born in Argyll. He was educated at Oxford where he was a brilliant student of languages. He taught himself Gaelic so successfully that he became one of the outstanding Gaelic poets of this century. He is one of the few poets who has been equally fluent in three languages English, Scots and Gaelic. He served in World War II in North Africa and this had a disturbing effect on his life and a profound influence on his poetry.

Do Bheithe Boidheach

Neul a' snàmh air an speur,
duilleach eadar e s mo shùil;
ùr bàrr-uaine gruag a' bheithe,
leug nan leitir cas mu 'n Lùib.

Oiteag tighinn bhàrr an tuim,
a' toirt fuinn as do dhos;
cruit na gaoithe do bhàrr teudach,
cuisleannan nan geug ri port.

Ailleagan nan glac so shìos,
sìodhbhrugh do na h-eòin do dhlùths,
thu 'gan tàladh as gach àirde,
iad a' teàrnadh ort le sunnd.

Ceileireadh s e binn binn,
seirm is seinn air a' chnoc,
nuair a chromas na h-eòin Shamhraidh
air do mheanglain s mil 'nan gob.

Is fhèarr na'n ceòl t' fhaicinn fhéin
air bhogadan réidh fo 'n chnap,
seang bàrr-snìomhain amlach ùrar,
is dealt 'na chùirnein air gach slait.

To a Bonny Birch Tree

A cloud drifting in the sky, leafage between it and my eye; fresh and green-crested are the tresses of the birch, jewel of the steep descents about the Bight.

A gentle breeze from the knowe wins music from your crest, harp of the wind is your stringed top as the tendrils of the boughs make melody.

Gem of the hollows down there, a fairy mound for the birds is your close-set fastness; you charming them out of every airt, and they stooping down on you with cheer.

Sweet, sweet the chorusing, carolling and singing on the hillock, when the birds of summer alight on your sprays with honey in their beaks.

Better than their music is to see yourself, gently nodding below the little scaur, slim and fresh, with crest enlaced and plaited, and beads of dew on every branch.

Luinneag

Hug ó hoireann ó,
gura fada, cian fada,
hug ó hoireann ó.

B' e gairbhe na gaoithe
chum an raoir mi 'nam chaithris.

Gaoth á deas air Loch Fìne,
teachd gu fiochar le tartar,

Na tuinn chaoirgheal mu Gharbhail,
neart na fairge s a farum.

Is ann an raoir a bha'n nuallan
'na mo chluasan s mi 'n Sasuinn.

Gu'n tig fuaim an Uillt Bheithe
eadar mise s mo chadal.

Abhainn nan Gillean s a gaoir aic'
bho Loch a' Chaorainn 'na cabhaig,

Lagan Ròaig s tràigh na Lùibe
eadar mo shùilean s mo leabhar,

Agus Rudha Clach an Tràghaidh
a' snàmh air a' bhalla.

It was the Hardness of the Wind

It was the hardness of the wind that kept me awake last night.
A wind from the south on Loch Fyne, coming fiercely with uproar.
Waves blazing with foam round Garvel, the might of the sea and its clangour.
Last night its roaring was in my ears, and I was in England.
The sound of the Birch Burn comes between me and my sleep.
Abhainn nan Gillean with its outcry, hastening from Loch a' Chaorainn.
Lagan Roaig and the strand of the Bight between my eyes and my book.
And Ebbing Stone Point swimming on the wall.

An Sealgair Agus an Aois

Cuing mo dhroma an aois a nis
    rib' mo choise, robach, liath:
fear thig eadar soills' is sùilean,
    fear thig eadar rùn is gnìomh.

Fàgaidh e am faillean crotach,
    fo gach dos 's e chuireas sgian,
is och, b' e 'm bàrr air gach miosguinn,
    tighinn eadar mi s an sliabh.

Thug e dhìom a' Chruach Chaorainn,
    s an gunna caol, san ealchainn shuas:
bhuin e dhìom mo neart, am mèirleach,
    dh'fhàg e mi gun làmh, gun luaths.

Na'n robh aige corp a ghlacainn,
    s na'n tachrainn ris leis fhéin sa' bheinn,
bhiodh saltairt ann is fraoch 'ga reubadh,
    is fuil air feur mu'n sgaradh sinn.

Age and the Hunter

Yoke of my neck, this Age comes o'er me
    snare of my feet, the grey, the still
between my eyes and the light he is standing,
    he stands between the deed and the will

There is the hand that warps the sapling,
    that sets the knife to the apple's root;
and, oh, 'twas the crown of all his malice
    to snatch the hill from beneath my foot.

He has taken from me the paths of the Cruach,
    he has rusted my gun like an autumn leaf,
he has taken away from me strength and laughter,
    and hand and foot, like a heartless thief.

If Age were a man that hands could grapple,
    and I could come on him secretly
up on the hill where no man passes,
    grass would be reddened or he went free.

Ceithir Gaothan Na h-Albann

M'oiteag cheòlmhor chaoin 'teachd deiseil 'nam bheitheach Samhraidh i,
mo stoirm chuain le dìle 'cur still 's gach alldan domh,
a' ghaoth tuath le cathadh sneachda 'nì dreachmhor beanntan domh,
a' ghaoth 'tha'g iomain m'fhaloisg earraich ri leathad ghleanntaichean.

Duilleach an tSamhraidh, tuil an Dàmhair, na cuithean s an àrdghaoth Earraich i;
dùrd na coille, bùirich eas, ùire'n tsneachda s an fhaloisg i;
tlàths is binneas, àrdan, misneach, fàs is sileadh nam frasan i;
anail mo chuirp, àrach mo thuigse, mo làmhan, m'uilt is m'anam i;
fad na bliadhna, ré gach ràidhe, gach là s gach ciaradh feasgair dhomh,
is i Alba nan Gall s nan Gàidheal is gàire, is blàths, is beatha dhomh.

The Four Winds of Scotland

My melodious gentle breeze blowing from southward in my Summer birchwood is she; my ocean storm, with downpour sending in headlong spate each burn for me; the North wind with driving snow that makes beautiful the hills for me; the wind that drives my Springtime muirburn up the slopes of glens is she.

The leaves of Summer, the spate of Autumn, the snowdrifts and the high Spring wind is she; the sough of the woodland, the roaring of waterfalls, the freshness of the snow and the heather ablaze is she; mild pleasantness and melody, angry pride and courage, growth and the pouring of the showers is she; breath of my body, nurture of my understanding, my hands, my joints and my soul is she. All year long, each season through, each day and each fall of dusk for me, it is Alba, Highland and Lowland, that is laughter and warmth and life for me.

Grunnd Na Mara

"Tha iad ann an grunnd na mara,
is cha b' e sud an rogha cala" —
rug sud orm o dh' fhalbh mo mhacan,
an cuilean a bhithinn 'ga thatadh,
a dheanadh gàire 'na mo ghlacaibh.
Thàinig an seann sgeul air a chasan.
Tha 'n speur ag ciaradh mu fheasgar,
goir aig na h-eòin air na sgeirean,
geumnaich a' chruidh a' teachd dhachaidh,
éigheach nan giullan anns a' bhaile,

s mi'm thurraman leam fhéin mu'n chagailt,
a' smuaineachadh air na bh' agam.
Chì mi do chòta air an tarran,
is, och! an tigh gun fhuaim, gun fhacal,
an stairsneach nach bi fuaim chas oirr',
an seòmar fàs s an leabaidh fhalamh.
Ma's e an osna théid fada,
cluinnear m'osnaich far an laigh thu
'nad chadal luasganach san fheamainn,
s na fuathan a' sìor dhol seachad,
cruthanna aognaidh na mara!
[*Am marbh a' bruidhinn*]
"Eisd, a bhean, is na bi rium,
is truimide mo dhìol do bhròn;
sgàin is leagh an long fo 'r buinn —
thriall an cuimhn' an cois an deò.
Lunnainn a mharbh mi,
a mhill an tsùil nach fhaca i.
Theagamh gu'm b' aithne dhomh thu,
sgùr an sàl mo chuimhne nis.
Tha mi air sabhd sa' chuan mhór;
Bu Domhnall mise an dé.
laigh do ghul orm 'na lòd,
ge b' e có thu, a bhean, éisd".

Mo losgadh, mhuinntir nan Eilean,
is daor a phàigh sibh mórachd Bhreatainn!

Thonder They Ligg

"Thonder they ligg* on the grund o the sea,   *lie*
nae the hyne* whaur they wald be."   *haven*
Siccan a thing has happenit me
sin my son's been gane. When he was wee
I dannlit the bairn like a whelpikie
and he leuch i ma airms richt cantilie.
It's the auld weird* nou I maun dree†.   *fate; † suffer*
The luft* grows derk, the sun gangs laigh,   *sky*
atour the skerries the sea-maws skreigh,
the rowtan kye come schauchlan* doun,   *trudging*
the laddies rant out-throu the toun;
but here I rock at the fire ma lane,
mindan o him I had that's gane.
I see your jacket on the heuk,

but the hous is lown in ilka neuk,
never a sound or a word i the room,
nae sclaffan o buits* on the threshart-stane,   * boots
the bed cauld and the chalmer toom*.   * empty
Gin it's the sych* that traivels far   * sigh
ye'll hear my sychan whaur ye are,
sleepan i the wrack, jundied* aye,   * rocked, jostled
wi ugsome* ferliest sooman‡ by,   * ugly; † monsters; ‡ swimming
the ghaistlie monsters o the sea.
"Wheesht, woman, wheesht, and deavena* me   * do not deafen
My wae's the mair to see ye greet.
The ship brak doun under our feet,
life gaed aff, and memorie wi 't.
London slew me, weary faa 't,
connacht* the een that never saw it.   * deceived
Aiblins* I was acquent wi you,   * perhaps
the saut has reingeit* my memorie nou.   * scoured
Here I stravaig* i the merchlesst faem,   * wander; † unbounded
yestreen Donald was my name.
The wecht o your wae liggs sair on me.
Woman, wheesht, whae'er ye be."

Sair the price maun be dounpitten
by the island-fowk for the greatness o Britain.

Atman

Rinn thu goid 'nad éiginn,
dh'fheuch thu breug gu faotainn as,
dhìt iad, chàin is chuip iad thu,
is chuir iad thu fo ghlais.

Bha'm beul onorach a dhìt thu
pladach, bideach 'sa ghnùis ghlais;
bha Ceartas sreamshùileach o sgrùdadh
a leabhar cunntais s iad sìor phailt.

Ach am beul a dhearbhadh breugach,
bha e modhail, éibhinn, binn;
fhuair mi eirmseachd is sgeòil uaith
s gun e ro eòlach air tràth bìdh.

Thogte do shùil o'n obair
á cruth an tsaoghail a dheoghal tlachd;
mhol thu Debel Iussuf dhomh,
a cumadh is a dath.

Is aithne dhomh thu, Atmain,
bean do thaighe s do chóignear òg,
do bhaidnein ghobhar is t'asail,
do ghoirtein seagail is do bhó.

Is aithne dhomh thu, Atmain;
is fear thu s tha thu beò,
dà nì nach eil am breitheamh,
s a chaill e 'chothrom gu bhith fòs.

Cha n-ainmig t'fhallus na do shùilean,
is eòl duit sùgradh agus fearg,
bhlais is bhlais thu'n difir
eadar milis agus searbh.

Dh'fheuch thu gràin is bròn is gàire,
dh'fheuch thu ànradh agus grian,
dh'fhairich thu a' bheatha
is cha do mheath thu roimpe riamh.

Na'n robh thu beairteach, is do chaolan
garbh le caoile t'airein sgìth,
cha bhiodh tu 'chuideachd air na mìolan
an dubh phrìosan Mhondovì.

Nuair gheibh breitheamh còir na cùirte
làn a shùla de mo dhruim,
thig mi a thaobh gu d'fhàilteachadh
trasd an tsràid ma chì mi thu.

Sidna Aissa, chaidh a cheusadh
mar ri mèirlich air bàrr sléibh,
is b'e'n toibheum, Atmain, àicheadh
gur bràthair dhomh thu fhéin.

Atman

You thieved in your need, and you tried a lie to get off. They condemned you, reviled you and whipped you, and they put you under lock and key.

The honourable mouth that condemned you was blubberish and tiny in the grey face; and Justice was blear-eyed from scrutinising its account-books, and they ever showing abundance.

But the mouth which was found lying was mannerly, cheerful and melodious; I got sharp repartee and tales from it, though it was not too well acquainted with a meal.

Your eye would be raised from your work to draw pleasure from the shape of the world; you praised Jebel Yussuf to me, its form and its colour.

I know you, Atman, the woman of your house and your five young things, your little clump of goats and your ass, your plot of rye and your cow.

I know you, Atman. You are a man, and you are alive; two things the judge is not, and that he has lost his chance of being ever.

Your sweat is not seldom in your eyes; you know what sporting and anger are; you have tasted and tasted the difference between sweet and bitter.

You have tried hatred and grief and laughter; you have tried tempest and sun; you have felt life and never shrunk before it.

Had you been wealthy, and your gut thick with the leanness of your tired ploughmen, you would not be keeping company with the lice in the black prison of Mondovi.

When the decent judge of the court gets the fill of his eye of my back, I will come aside to welcome you across the street if I see you.

Sidna Aissa (Our Lord Jesus) was crucified along with thieves on the top of a hill, and it would be blasphemy, Atman, to deny that you are a brother of mine.

Truaighe Na h-Eorpa

Tha mùir shnaidhte na h-Eòrpa
    shìos 'nan tòrr air a raointean.

Tha an gràbhaladh àrsaidh
    air a sgàineadh is gaorr air.

Tha dlùthshreathan a tùirean
    'nam mionsprùidhlich air aomadh.

Tha muinntir a tallachan
    sgapte air faontra.

Is luaineach, làn airce,
    oidhch' is latha a daoine.

Chaidh geurghuth an truaighe.
thar cruaidhghàir a gaothan.

Dh'fhalbh bharr na h-Eòrpa
trian de 'bòidhchead sèimh aosda.

Sean tearmunn na h-ealain,
cridhe meachair na daondachd.

Och, Rudha na h-Aisia,
Bàlcan an t-saoghail!

Europe's Piteous Plight

The finely hewn ramparts of Europe are down in a heap upon her plains.
  Their ancient carvings are split and scattered.
  The close-fitting courses of her towers are collapsed in small rubble.
  The people of her halls are wanderers dispersed.
  Without ever rest, full of need, are the nights and days of her folk.
  The shrill voice of their pitiful complaining drowns the hard roaring of her winds.
  Gone from Europe is a third of her tranquil, aged beauty.
  The old sanctuary of the arts, the tender heart of humanity.
  Och, she is become a promontory of Asia, the Balkans of the world!

An t-Iasgair

So mar dh'aithnich mi riamh thu,
fhuair oilein aig sgoil an iasgaich.

An sealladh fìr, na sùilean socrach
a sgrùdadh slugan dubh an doininn,
s a leughadh seagh an àrdthuinn obainn,
ceann geal troimh dhall na h-oidhche 'nochdadh.

Tha fuaradh s fasgadh, faire s fulang
'nad shùil s an ciùine do ghutha;
dh'fhàg caol is cuan, rudh' air rudha
le'n sruthan-cinn s an gaothaibh uile,
dh'fhàg cathadh sguabte iomadh tuinne,
fèath is gaillionn is sìontan dubha,
air do ghruaidh an seul, a dhuine.

The Fisherman

This is how I ever recognised you, who were brought up at the school of the fishing.

The man's look, the steady eyes that would search the black gullet of the storm; that would read the meaning of the sudden towering wave, a white crest showing through the blindness of the night.

Windward and leeward, watching and enduring are in your eye and in the gentleness of your voice. Kyle and open ocean, foreland after foreland with their head tides and all their winds have left their imprint on you; the swept spindrift of many a wave, calm and gale and black tempest have set their seal upon your cheek, man.

Bisearta

Chi mi rè geàrd na h-oidhche
dreòs air chrith 'na fhroidhneas thall air fàire,
ag clapail le a sgiathaibh,
a' sgapadh s ag ciaradh rionnagan na h-àird' ud.

Shaoileadh tu gu'n cluinnte,
ge cian, o 'bhuillsgein ochanaich no caoineadh,
ràn corruich no gàir fuatha,
comhart chon cuthaich uaidh no ulfhairt fhaolchon;
gu'n ruigeadh drannd an fhòirneirt
o'n fhùirneis òmair iomall fhéin an tsaoghail.
Ach sud a' dol an leud e
ri oir an speur an tosdachd olc is aognuidh.

C'ainm an nochd a th'orra,
na sràidean bochda anns an sgeith gach uinneag
a lasraichean s a deatach,
a sradagan is sgreadail a luchd thuinidh,
is taigh air thaigh 'ga reubadh
am broinn a chéile am brùchdadh toit' a' tuiteam?
Is có an nochd tha'g atach
am Bàs a theachd gu grad 'nan cainntibh uile,
no a' spàirn measg chlach is shailthean
air bháinidh ag gairm air cobhair, is nach cluinnear?
Có an nochd a phàigheas
sean chìs àbhaisteach na fala cumant?

Uair dearg mar lod na h-àraich,
uair bán mar ghile thràighte an eagail éitigh,
a' dìreadh s uair a' teàrnadh,
a' sìneadh le sitheadh àrd s ag call a mheudachd,
a' fannachadh car aitil
s ag at mar anail dhiabhail air dhéinead,
an t-Olc 'na chridhe s 'na chuisle,
chì mi 'na bhuillean a' sìoladh s a' leum e.
Tha'n dreòs 'na oillt air fàire,
'na fhàinne ròis is òir am bun nan speuran,
a' breugnachadh s ag àicheadh
le' shoillse sèimhe àrsaidh àrd nan reultan.

Bizerta

I see during the night guard a blaze flickering, fringing the skyline over yonder, beating with its wings and scattering and dimming the stars of that airt.

You would think that there would be heard from its midst, though far away, wailing and lamentation, the roar of rage and the yell of hate, the barking of the dogs from it or the howling of wolves, that the snarl of violence would reach from yon amber furnace the very edge of the world; but yonder it spreads along the rim of the sky in evil ghastly silence.

What is their name to-night, the poor streets where every window spews its flame and smoke, its sparks and the screaming of its inmates; while house upon house is rent and caves in in a gust of smoke? And who to-night are beseeching death to come quickly in all their tongues, or are struggling among stones and beams, crying in frenzy for help, and are not heard? Who to-night is paying the old accustomed tax of common blood?

Now red like a battlefield puddle, now pale like the drained whiteness of foul fear, climbing and sinking, reaching and darting up and shrinking in size, growing faint for a moment and swelling like the breath of a devil in intensity, I see Evil as a pulse and a heart declining and leaping in throbs. The blaze, a horror on the skyline, a ring of rose and gold at the foot of the sky, belies and denies with its light the ancient high tranquillity of the stars.

The Old Fisherman

Greet the bights that gave me shelter,
they will hide me no more with the horns of their forelands.
I peer in a haze, my back is stooping;
my dancing days for fishing are over.

The shoot that was straight in the wood withers,
the bracken shrinks red in the rain and shrivels,
the eyes that would gaze in the sun waver;
my dancing days for fishing are over.

The old boat must seek the shingle,
her wasting side hollow the gravel,
the hand that shakes must leave the tiller;
my dancing days for fishing are over.

The sea was good night and morning,
the winds were friends, the calm was kindly —
the snow seeks the burn, the brown fronds scatter;
my dancing days for fishing are over.

The Hind of Morning

She snorts and stamps upon the eastern hill,
the Hind of Morning, longing for the day,
the Hind of Morning, mad to leap away,
and flings her head up, scorning to be still.

On high her hooves strike up a streaming fire,
that wavers, slanting past the haloed peaks;
her quick feet spurn the summits, and she seeks
to trample night and burn it up entire.

The Hind of Morning leaps and will not stay,
she stretches West and West with flinging stride,
the Hind of Morning pacing in her pride,
the Hind of Morning is away, away.

At the Quayside

The buyers peer with hands in pockets,
black against the break of day,
and reinge their wits for jests to cheapen
our siller won from waters grey.
Down from the quay they climb to finger
what our brown nets swept away,
the hard-won harvest we have wrestled
from sea and night, from wind and spray.

What do they know, or any others
of how the midnight wind commands,
and herds the glimmering crests to leeward
to break in ranks on hidden strands,
or how dawn shows the torn horizon
to staring eyes or frozen hands?
Only the night sea, wudd with winter,
can give them the mind that understands.

We weather foreland after foreland,
and string the bow of every bight,
where lamps in homes by windless harbours
shine warm and yellow through the night.
We face, unshielded, wind and water,
and black to leeward as we fight
we glimpse the crouching, thundering forelands
that bare their fangs there, foaming white.

Hour and hour the hammering motor
echoes through the hold below;
hour and hour the restless forefoot
soars, then belts the black to snow;
the dark sea, wounded, phosphorescent,
lashes, with icy fire aglow,
the eyes that read it, watching forward
the sliding waters as we go.

Our wives at home are waking with us.
Listening to the gale they lie.
We listen to its high crests hissing,
and mark the neighbour's light outbye,

red now, green now, lifting, sinking,
while, unquiet, our steerman's eye
traces the stays to where the masthead
staggers its arc across the sky.

And lights on one bright star beyond it,
above a cloudrim winking plain
like a beacon on a rampart,
and of a sudden sees it wane.
Down the wind a grey wall marches,
towering; across us leap again
the streaming spindrift and the fury,
the squall, the blindness and the rain.

And if Fortune chances on us
in the dark, and swings our keel
into the airt where shoals are swimming,
we mark them, shoot and round them wheel.
Then a foot for purchase on the gunnel,
numb hands that have lost their feel,
the ebb tide straining, the steep seas snatching
a backrope like a rod of steel.

The buyers outlined on the quayside
ganting and peering in a line,
the half-awakened early risers
that wonder if the night was fine,
though they can look at dark to seaward,
and see far out our torches shine,
what can they know of our dim battles
round Pladda, Arran and Loch Fyne?

Maurice Lindsay

Maurice Lindsay has had a long fruitful career as poet, anthologist, editor, and historian of Scottish literature. Like that of Louis MacNeice, his poetry has a rough generous 'feel' of reality, aspects of people and places being caught as it were 'on the wing'. His sympathies are wide and his humanity warm. His knowledge of and insight into music are specially worthy of mention.

I have always been an 'occasional' poet, in the sense that a moment of lyrical intensity, sudden insight into a character, the shock of a public happening or a phrase in a newspaper or in conversation, can set off in my imagination the process that may perhaps eventually result in a poem. 'The chief, perhaps the only aim of poetry, is delight' Dryden declared. Taking 'delight' in its widest sense, to include the incongruities that produce humour and that sense of *frisson* which come through a sense of horror or pity, I would agree with him.

I do not think it is the job of the poet to seek to emulate the Post Office or British Telecom in the transmission of messages. Nor do I think poetry should emulate religions or politics in purveying dogma. Both produce at best partial interpretations of the truth and — except possibly in the case of protest poetry by writers suffering under oppressive tyrannies such as those exercised in South Africa and in countries under Marxist rule — are usually invoked to evade the need for a genuine poetic resolution; one wrested from the imagination.

Having been trained originally as a musician, I like poetry which respects musical values. Rhyme and traditional forms still seem to me to be capable of being used in new and personal ways. Free verse, though no longer thought mandatory (any more than abstraction is in painting), needs to have a firmly controlled central balancing point if it is not simply to collapse into chopped-up prose.

Above all, I have always striven to deserve the title a reviewer in the *Times Literary Supplement* bestowed upon me many years ago; that of being 'an enjoyable poet'.

Maurice Lindsay was born in Glasgow in 1918 and educated at Glasgow Academy and what is now the Royal Scottish Academy of Music and Drama, before serving as an officer with the Cameronians (Scottish Rifles) during the War.

He then embarked on a career as a broadcaster in radio and, later, also television. He was Music Critic of the Glasgow newspaper *The Bulletin* from 1946 to 1961, in which year he became Programme Controller of Border Television in Carlisle. In 1967 he was appointed the first Director of the Scottish Civic Trust.

His first twelve books of verse are now represented by his *Collected Poems* (Paul Harris, Edinburgh, 1974). His subsequent books are *A Net to Catch the Wind* (Hale, 1981) and *The French Mosquitoes' Woman and Other Diversions and Poems* (Hale, 1985).

London, September 1940

Helplessly the wavering searchlights probe
    where stuttering bombers fly:
each thud and flash their faceless pilots lob,
    anonymous numbers die,
shaking a length of protest from the ground:
    ack-ack guns chatter,
more distant heavies boom, and make resound
    the emptiness they batter.

Watching these beams meet in the cloudy blue
    of this unsummered night's
bewildered terror, foolishly, it's you
    who lingers in my sights,
eyes wide upon *Les Sylphides*. I remember
    you sitting at my side
through the uneasiness of that September
    when thought of peace died,

the sway of whiteness as the music dreamed
   what only music knows;
joy, more intense since it already seemed
   lost in our long-agos:
applause; the broken spell; cheer upon cheer
   for delicate civilisation,
as if the audience sensed that they'd been near
   some final consummation:
the heavy curtain tumbling from the ceiling;
   the glow of the house lights;
lifting a fur around your shoulders, feeling
   love must set all to rights:

helping you rise; the popping-back of your seat;
   a statue's marble stare;
your clinging little shudder as we met
   a coldly threatening air;
the newsboy hoarsely calling — *Hitler speaks;*
   the separating fear
of distance, blanched like powder on your cheeks
   at the mere thought of war . . .

Now it has happened. Searchlights take the sky,
and naked in another's arms you lie.

Jock, the Laird's Brother

Strutting across the red moors of his memory, Jock, the Laird's brother,
tingling, tweedy bagpipe trousers, whisky map-veined face,
under his arm a leering gun, the image of his father,
the skirling tradition of fishes and pheasants, the ownership of space;

the purple, peopleless moors of Scotland where poverty seeds in the ground,
and love turns grey as the ashy, prickled, bleak-burned skeletoned heather,
where sleek guns splutter their patter in August, and gasping grouse are found
on the noses of snuffling dogs, and the hills are always the talk of weather.

Once, he was keeper of animals claimed from God to be owned by a Scottish
    lord;
once, he patrolled the edges of forests, a poacher's pleasure his full despair;
now, he is grown the villagers' measure with his regular walks, an old man,
    absurd,
with the look of one who's been left behind by thoughts that were never there.

Picking Apples

Apple time, and the trees brittle with fruit.
My children climb the bent, half-sapping branches
to where the apples, cheeked with the hectic flush
of Autumn, hang. The children bark their haunches

and lean on the edge of their balance. The apples are out
of reach; so they shake the tree. Through a tussle of leaves and laughter
the apples thud down; thud on the orchard grasses
in rounded, grave finality, each one after

the other dropping; the muffled sound of them dropping
like suddenly hearing the beats of one's own heart
falling away, as if shaken by some storm
as localised as this. Loading them into the cart,

the sweet smell of their bruises moist in the sun,
their skin's bloom tacky against the touch,
I experience fulfilment, suddenly aware
of some ripe, wordless answer, knowing no such

answers exist; only questions, questions, the beating years,
the dropped apples . . . the kind of touch and go
that poetry makes satisfaction of;
reality, with nothing more to show

than a brush of branches, time and the apples falling,
and shrill among the leaves, children impatiently calling.

Aged Four

Alone beside himself, head-in-air
he wanders gently through a fading season,
almost for the last time aware
of how a moment feels, before the lesion

of growing into thought begin to hurt;
the falling burn turn into a complaint
it can't communicate; earth on the hands be dirt
that rubs a sudden scolding up; each feint

the wind boxes the trees with, trace a why
nobody answers; rain be more than wet;
clouds that unfold each other, shape a sky
forecasting portent. Head-in-air, and yet

reluctant to come in, he stands and bawls,
sensing from how much loss his mother calls.

June Rain

For days the sun had slaked the fields with heat.
Walking the dusty roadway, whitened feet
gritted your breathing's edge. A cricket's beat

scratched on the hayfield stooks its brittle rune.
Not even the spongy shadow of the moon
rubbed out the lazing fever of that June.

And then, one afternoon, came sudden rain.
It slapped and rattled, like a lengthy train
distantly clanking trucks across a plain.

It stroked and soaked each clotted run of earth,
while farmers reckoned up what it was worth,
and politicians claimed they'd staved off dearth.

The scented hedgerows glistened. New light stirred
in trees and bushes. Here and there, a bird
picked up clean notes and tuned them, freshly heard.

The Tunnel

(A Bairnsang)

I wuldna gae near thon tunnel gin I was you,
for losh, it's a muckle great dragon's gantan mou!

Frae faur and near, it sooks in screaman trains;
an eftir it's swallow't them hail, you can hear its pains.

It burps out smeik and soot when it's jist had its fill,
but when it gets hungry, it liggs that quate and still.

I wouldna gae near thon dragonish tunnel the nou,
for it's no had a train for hoors, and it micht eat you!

Farm Woman

She left the warmth of her body tucked round her man
before first light, for the byre, where mist and the moist
hot breath of the beasts half-hid the electric veins
of the milking machines. Later, she'd help to hoist
the heavy cans for the tractor to trundle down
to the farm-road end, while her raw hands scoured the dairy.
By seven o'clock, she'd have breakfast on the table,
her kitchen bright as her apron pin, the whole house airy.
Her men-folk out in the fields, the children off to school,
she'd busy herself with the house and the hens. No reasons
clouded the other side of the way she brought
to her man the generous amplitude of the seasons.

Not much of a life, they'd whisper at church soirées
as they watched her chat, her round face buttered with content,
unable to understand that for her each moment
rubbed out the one before, and simply lent
nothing for words of theirs to touch to argument.

School Prizegiving

The voice rose out of his enormous paunch
reverberant with wisdom rounded there
since he had stood, a sliver of himself,
with boys like these in some lost otherwhere

innumerable platitudes away.
And yet, for all its width, the voice was small,
smooth-feathered still, cock-crested in success
that time had caponed, centre of the hall.

And as his little meanings strutted out
in preening words, the eager fledgling boys
who listened must have wondered if they too
might one day make the same wing-beating noise

to keep their courage up, their run of years
inexplicably fouled, their hopeful hastes
turned back upon themselves; each still so sure
he'd force his way beyond these middle wastes . . .

And I, aware how satisfaction breaks
against its realisation, and how thick
the darkness gathers, caught myself, ashamed,
half-murmuring: *Their prizes, masters, quick!*

At Hans Christian Andersen's Birthplace, Odense, Denmark

Sunlight folds back pages of quiet shadows
against the whitewashed walls of his birthplace. Tourists move
through crowded antiseptic rooms and ponder
what row after row of glass-cased papers ought to prove.

Somehow the long-nosed gangling boy who was only
at home in fairyland, has left no clues.
The tinder-box of Time we rub
answers us each the way we choose.

For kings have now no daughters left for prizes.
Swineherds must remain swineherds; and no spell
can make the good man prince; psychiatrists
have dredged up wonder from the wishing well.

The whole of his terrible, tiny world might be
dismissed as a beautiful madman's dream, but that each of us knows
whenever we move out from the warmth of our loneliness
we may be wearing the Emperor's new clothes.

Small Boy Writing

My little son beside me shapes his letters,
a tremulous M, a not-quite-meeting O,
sticking them with his breath down careful pages,
row on repeated row.

He'll heir the questions elder, self-styled betters
have jumbled from these same laborious signs,
and find what somehow answered for their ages
has slipped between the lines:

their lingered creeds and dogmas, slackened fetters
no longer strong enough to hold the mind
back from its baffled necessary sieges,
though nothing's there behind.

He'll find how little we are still their debtors,
their purposes unpurposed, doubts secured
without assurances, their faith's self-pledges,
    lonelinesses endured.

So may he learn resistance to go-getters
prospecting ends and absolutes; be content
to take delight's quick shapes and sudden edges
    as living's monument.

Speaking of Scotland

What do you mean when you speak of Scotland?
The grey defeats that are dead and gone
behind the legends each generation
savours afresh, yet can't live on?

Lowland farms with their broad acres
peopling crops? The colder earth
of the North East? Or Highland mountains
shouldering up their rocky dearth?

Inheritance of guilt that our country
has never stood where we feel she should?
A nagging threat of unfinished struggle
somehow forever lost in the blood?

Scotland's a sense of change, an endless
becoming for which there was never a kind
of wholeness or ultimate category.
Scotland's an attitude of mind.

Love's Anniversaries

(for Joyce)

It was the generosity of delight
that first we learned in a sparsely-furnished flat
clothed in our lovers' nakedness. By night
we timidly entered what we marvelled at,

ranging the flesh's compass. But by day
we fell together, fierce with awkwardness
that window-light and scattered clothing lay
impassive round such urgent happiness.

Now, children, years and many rooms away,
and tired with experience, we climb the stairs
to our well-furnished room; undress, and say
familiar words for love; and from the cares

that back us, turn together and once more seek
the warmth of wonder each to the other meant
so strong ago, and with known bodies speak
the unutterable language of content.

Two Generations

A twig cracked, no louder than
a bone snapped in a furred trap.
Rabbits can't size fear. One flopped
across our harmless track slap

into the blue bolt a stoat
launched from a farm gate.
Fangs fastened the neck's shriek,
a cold killing without hate.

Stop it, the child cried: *Oh, why don't you stop it?*
face to face with what has no stop,
and the useless pity that brought down
the back of my hand in a sharp chop.

Travelling Folk

Cornered in wastes of land, spinnies of old roads
lopped back from the new, where done horses
leant once on starved haunches, battered cars
nuzzle scrunted bushes and caravans.

Copper-breasted women suckle defiance
at schools inspectors. Sanitary men
are met with bronze-age scowls. All to no purpose.
Blown across Europe's centuries, bound only

in piths and withies to settlements not moved
by permanent impermanencies — smokey
violins, dusks gathered from skies
purple as hedge-fruits, or plucked stolen chickens —

these exiles from our human order seed
in the rough, overlooked verges of living,
their stubborn litter filling with vagrancy,
the cracks our need for conformation shows.

Anon

They are excavating the mound at the foot of the village,
young men with gentle eyes and curious beards,
and names like Brown and Soutar, and soft-breasted girls
on whom they'll one day stamp their borrowed image,
name upon name. What else have they to preserve?

They are digging for signs. How like were the other Browns
and Soutars, ripening out of the blameless soil,
and having to leave their names when it took them under?
Turning over the freshly wounded earth,
only Anon stares out from whitened bone.

Of Skunks and Men

The Common Skunk, men call me:
    I do not understand
why for my coat they maul me,
    yet mock my anal gland.

That smelly, yellow evil
    I squirt from bushy tail
is surely no less civil
    than what their tongues exhale?

I stink to gain protection
    from bigger beasts than me;
their words are a projection
    of how they disagree.

While all men are injected
    with lies the other tells,
we skunks are not affected:
    each knows the other smells.

Mozart's Salzburg

Age after age this rock that reared a castle
where Prince-Archbishops staved time and its wars at bay,
grew stately halls on stems of corridors
that now drain back their legends. Day after day

guides patter up the ghosts of pleasured men
whom splendour dignified with destiny; turned cold,
their comfortless pomp now clothed in fountained stone:
men without *pietas*, most of them utterly loathed.

We are shepherded to where the past stopped
for this place. Napoleon broke the spell
of gracious iron blessings: the last Archbishop
gathered his robes and fled, the guides tell

us in several languages. Yet who would care
what made one tyranny different from another
if a man with staring eyes and backstair jokes
hadn't served up music that small-talk couldn't smother;

a fellow too big for his boots who didn't seem worth his pay,
sounding his age to agelessness, beyond the reach of their say.

W. S. Graham

W. S. Graham, one of the outstanding British poets of our time, died in January 1986 after a long illness. Brought up in working-class Greenock, he left school early taking a mechanical-engineering apprenticeship, a most unlikely background for a leading poet in the Apocalypse Movement. His intricate idiosyncratic style has clarified itself over the years and his main subject is seen as a poetic exploration of the possibilities of communication. Alongside these poems however there are ones of place and people — such as the ones about Greenock — which are among the most beautiful and exhilarating in Scottish poetry.

In the Poetry Book Society Bulletins of Spring 1970 and Autumn 1977, W. S. Graham has some valuable things to say about his poetry, and in particular his two collections *Malcolm Mooney's Land* and *Implements in Their Places*. In his observations on the former book, he writes:

Thoughts of the process of making poetry are often the subject of my poems, although I hope the poem is left standing in its own right apart from any take-awayable message the reader might discover.

I happen to feel most alive when I am trying to write poetry. So here I am battering against the door in case there might be somebody behind it.

I am always very aware that my poem is not a telephone call. The poet only speaks one way. He hears nothing back. His words as he utters them are not conditioned by a real ear replying from the other side. That is why he has to make the poem stand stationary as an Art object. He never knows who will collide with it and maybe even use it as a different utensil from what he intended. Yet because I am only human, I hope I am in it somewhere.

With regard to *Implements in Their Places*
he writes:

I can discern maybe an effort somewhere to try to be more simple or, if
you will, less confused by the English language. But the word 'simple' is
difficult either applied to lines of words on the page or to the thought
which provoked them. Maybe this book is going to be more entertaining
to more people. Is that what I want? After speaking to myself I suppose I
want to speak to the best, whoever they are, alive or dead.

W. S. Graham was born in Greenock in 1918. He served his apprenticeship as an
engineer. His first book of poems was published in 1942; an early reputation was gained
with the publication of the *Nightfishing* in 1955. A number of volumes and his *Collected
Poems* (1977) have followed. He has given readings of his work in this country and
America and has lectured in New York University. He lived with his wife, also
Scottish, in Cornwall for many years.

Listen. Put on Morning

Listen. Put on morning.
Waken into falling light.
A man's imagining
Suddenly may inherit
The handclapping centuries
Of his one minute on earth.
And hear the virgin juries
Talk with his own breath
To the corner boys of his street.
And hear the Black Maria
Searching the town at night.
And hear the playropes caa
The sister Mary in.
And hear Willie and Davie
Among bracken of Narnain
Sing in a mist heavy
With myrtle and listeners.
And hear the higher town

Weep a petition of fears
At the poorhouse close upon
The public heartbeat.
And hear the children tig
And run with my own feet
Into the netting drag
Of a suiciding principle.
Listen. Put on lightbreak.
Waken into miracle.
The audience lies awake
Under the tenements
Under the sugar docks
Under the printed moments.
The centuries turn their locks
And open under the hill

Their inherited books and doors
All gathered to distil
Like happy berry pickers
One voice to talk to us.
Yes listen. It carries away
The second and the years
Till the heart's in a jacket of snow
And the head's in a helmet white
And the song sleeps to be wakened
By the morning ear bright.
Listen. Put on morning.
Waken into falling light.

From: The Nightfishing

Shooting the Nets

It is us at last sailed into the chance
Of a good take. For there is the water gone
Lit black and wrought like iron into the look
That's right for herring. We dropped to the single motor.
The uneasy and roused gulls slid across us with
Swelled throats screeching. Our eyes sharpened what
Place we made through them. Now almost the light
To shoot the nets,

And keep a slow headway. One last check
To the gear. Our mended newtanned nets, all ropes
Loose and unkinked, tethers and springropes fast,
The tethers generous with floats to ride high,
And the big white bladder floats at hand to heave.
The bow wakes hardly a spark at the black hull.
The night and day both change their flesh about
In merging levels.

No more than merely leaning on the sea
We move. We move on this near-stillness enough
To keep the rudder live and gripped in the keel-wash.
We're well hinted herring plenty for the taking,
About as certain as all those signs falling
Through their appearance. Gulls settle lightly forward
Then scare off wailing as the sea-dusk lessens
Over our stern.

Yes, we're right set, see, see them go down, the best
Fishmarks, the gannets. They wheel high for a moment
Then heel, slip off the bearing air to plummet
Into the schooling sea. It's right for shooting,
Fish breaking the oiled water, the sea still
Holding its fires. Right, easy ahead, we'll run
Them straight out lined to the west. Now they go over,
White float and rope

And the net fed out in arm-lengths over the side.
So we shoot out the slowly diving nets
Like sowing grain. There they drag back their drifting
Weight out astern, a good half-mile of corks
And bladders. The last net's gone and we make fast
And cut the motor. The corks in a gentle wake,
Over curtains of water, tether us stopped, lapped
At far last still.

It is us no more moving, only the mere
Maintaining levels as they mingle together.
Now round the boat, drifting its drowning curtains
A grey of light begins. These words take place.
The petrel dips at the water-fats. And quietly
The stillness makes its way to its ultimate home.
The bilges slap. Gulls wail and settle.
It is us still.

From: The Nightfishing

Hauling the Catch

> We are at the hauling then hoping for it
> The hard slow haul of a net white with herring
> Meshed hard. I haul, using the boat's cross-heave
> We've started, holding fast as we rock back,
> Taking slack as we go to. The day rises brighter
> Over us and the gulls rise in a wailing scare
> From the nearest net-floats. And the unfolding water
> Mingles its dead.
>
> Now better white I can say what's better sighted,
> The white net flashing under the watched water,
> The near net dragging back with the full belly
> Of a good take certain, so drifted easy
> Slow down on us or us hauled up upon it
> Curved in a garment down to thicker fathoms.
> The hauling nets come in sawing the gunwale
> With herring scales.
>
> The air bunches to a wind and roused sea-cries.
> The weather moves and stoops high over us and
> There the forked tern, where my look's whetted on distance,
> Quarters its hunting sea. I haul slowly
> Inboard the drowning flood as into memory,
> Braced at the breathside in my net of nerves.
> We haul and drift them home. The winds slowly
> Turn round on us and
>
> Gather towards us with dragging weights of water
> Sleekly swelling across the humming sea
> And gather heavier. We haul and hold and haul
> Well the bright chirpers home, so drifted whitely
> All a blinding garment out of the grey water.
> And, hauling hard in the drag, the nets come in,
> The headrope a sore pull and feeding its brine
> Into our hacked hands.

Over the gunwale over into our deep lap
The herring come in, staring from their scales,
Fruitful as our deserts would have it out of
The deep and shifting seams of water. We haul
Against time fallen ill over the gathering
Rush of the sea together. The calms dive down.
The strident kingforked airs roar in their shell.
We haul the last

Net home and the last tether off the gathering
Run of the started sea. And then was the first
Hand at last lifted getting us swung against
Into the homing quarter, running that white grace
That sails me surely ever away from home.
And we hold into it as it moves down on
Us running white on the hull heeled to light.
Our bow heads home

Into the running blackbacks soaring us loud
High up in open arms of the towering sea.
The steep bow heaves, hung on these words, towards
What words your lonely breath blows out to meet it.
It is the skilled keel itself knowing its own
Fathoms it further moves through, with us there
Kept in its common timbers, yet each of us
Unwound upon

By a lonely behaviour of the all common ocean.
I cried headlong from my dead. The long rollers,
Quick on the crests and shirred with fine foam,
Surge down then sledge their green tons weighing dead
Down on the shuddered deck-boards. And shook off
All that white arrival upon us back to falter
Into the waking spoil and to be lost in
The mingling world.

The Constructed Space

Meanwhile surely there must be something to say,
Maybe not suitable but at least happy
In a sense here between us two whoever
We are. Anyhow here we are and never

Before have we two faced each other who face
Each other now across this abstract scene
Stretching between us. This is a public place
Achieved against subjective odds and then
Mainly an obstacle to what I mean.

It is like that, remember. It is like that
Very often at the beginning till we are met
By some intention risen up out of nothing.
And even then we know what we are saying
Only when it is said and fixed and dead.
Or maybe, surely, of course we never know
What we have said, what lonely meanings are read
Into the space we make. And yet I say
This silence here for in it I might hear you.

I say this silence or, better, construct this space
So that somehow something may move across
The caught habits of language to you and me.
From where we are it is not us we see
And times are hastening yet, disguise is mortal.
The times continually disclose our home.
Here in the present tense disguise is mortal.
The trying times are hastening. Yet here I am
More truly now this abstract act become.

I leave this at your ear

For Nessie Dunsmuir

I leave this at your ear for when you wake,
A creature in its abstract cage asleep.
Your dreams blindfold you by the light they make.

The owl called from the naked-woman tree
As I came down by the Kyle farm to hear
Your house silent by the speaking sea.

I have come late but I have come before
Later with slaked steps from stone to stone
To hope to find you listening for the door.

I stand in the ticking room. My dear, I take
A moth kiss from your breath. The shore gulls cry.
I leave this at your ear for when you wake.

Loch Thom

1

Just for the sake of recovering
I walked backward from fifty-six
Quick years of age wanting to see,
And managed not to trip or stumble
To find Loch Thom and turned round
To see the stretch of my childhood
Before me. Here is the loch. The same
Long-beaked cry curls across
The heather-edges of the water held
Between the hills a boyhood's walk
Up from Greenock. It is the morning.

And I am here with my mammy's
Bramble jam scones in my pocket.
The Firth is miles and I have come
Back to find Loch Thom maybe
In this light does not recognise me.

This is a lonely freshwater loch.
No farms on the edge. Only
Heather grouse-moor stretching
Down to Greenock and One Hope
Street or stretching away across
Into the blue moors of Ayrshire.

2

And almost I am back again
Wading the heather down to the edge
To sit. The minnows go by in shoals
Like iron-filings in the shallows.

My mother is dead. My father is dead
And all the trout I used to know
Leaping from their sad rings are dead.

3

I drop my crumbs into the shallow
Weed for the minnows and pinheads.
You see that I will have to rise
And turn round and get back where
My running age will slow for a moment
To let me on. It is a colder
Stretch of water than I remember.

The curlew's cry travelling still
Kills me fairly. In front of me
The grouse flurry and settle. GOBACK
GOBACK GOBACK FAREWELL LOCH THOM.

To Alexander Graham

Lying asleep walking
Last night I met my father
Who seemed pleased to see me.
He wanted to speak. I saw
His mouth saying something
But the dream had no sound.

We were surrounded by
Laid-up paddle steamers
In The Old Quay in Greenock.
I smelt the tar and the ropes.

It seemed that I was standing
Beside the big iron cannon
The tugs used to tie up to
When I was a boy. I turned
To see Dad standing just
Across the causeway under
That one lamp they keep on.

He recognised me immediately.
I could see that. He was
The handsome, same age
With his good brows as when
He would take me on Sundays
Saying we'll go for a walk.

Dad, what am I doing here?
What is it I am doing now?
Are you proud of me?
Going away, I knew
You wanted to tell me something.

You stopped and almost turned back
To say something. My father,
I try to be the best
In you you give me always.

Lying asleep turning
Round in the quay-lit dark
It was my father standing
As real as life. I smelt
The quay's tar and the ropes.

I think he wanted to speak.
But the dream had no sound.
I think I must have loved him.

Falling into the Sea

Breathing water is easy
If you put your mind to it.
The little difficulty
Of the first breath
Is soon got over. You
Will find everything right.

Keep your eyes open
As you go fighting down
But try to keep it easy
As you meet the green
Skylight rising up
Dying to let you through.

Then you will seem to want
To stand like a sea-horse
In the new suspension.
Dont be frightened. Breathe
Deeply and you will go down
Blowing your silver worlds.

Now you go down turning
Slowly over from fathom
To fathom even remembering
Unexpected small
Corners of the dream
You have been in. Now

What has happened to you?

You have arrived on the sea
Floor and a lady comes out
From the Great Kelp Wood
And gives you scones and a cup
Of tea and asks you
If you come here often.

Derick Thomson

Derick Thomson, Professor of Celtic at Glasgow University, is one of the leading contemporary Gaelic poets. As scholar, editor of the quarterly magazine *Gairm*, and author of many articles on Gaelic literature and history he has done as much for the Gaelic cause as anyone now living.

For those interested in further exploration of Gaelic literature his *An Introduction to Gaelic Poetry* (Victor Gollancz Ltd) is of great importance.

I was writing verse in Gaelic and English from my early teens, but finally settled down to using Gaelic only from my mid-twenties. But there was already some demand for English versions of Gaelic poems, and this has continued. It is an interesting index of Gaelic's place now in the Scottish literary scene, and I am glad that Gaelic has this extended public.

Already, over forty years ago, it seemed to me important to record, using the sort of intuition and observation a poet has, the Gaelic society I knew in Lewis, and the changes that were taking place. As time went on the focus for this observation became wider, and of course other experiences and views became important, but for many years that central interest attracted me strongly. It has led me to lyrical celebration and to depression and satire, and I never know where next it will lead.

My life's experience is made up of many ingredients: sensuous memory, personal relationships, love of place and its history, love of country, literary experience, scholarship, politics, practical activities. There is no end to what one may write about. I would like to think that I reacted sensitively and honestly to a good range of experiences, and put accurate labels on some of them.

I practise no religion, though I retain great admiration for many people who did. I have been a Nationalist for almost as long as I can remember. But I believe that we should aim at the same time at being much better Europeans than we are, and take a humble interest in the world as a whole.

Gaelic has had a long and intense poetic tradition which is very varied. It is exciting to belong to such a tradition. My own work over the years has developed freer styles of verse than are the norm in Gaelic, but inevitably it meshes with that long verse tradition, and gathers nuances from it. It has also been open to influences from other poetic traditions. All this probably makes for a greater complexity than appears on the surface.

I find myself torn between somewhat opposing views: that there is a particularity we should rejoice in, as Scots, Gaels or individuals, and that there is an identity that we share, whatever race or country or language we own. I make the best of believing both these propositions.

Derick Thomson (b. 1921), born in Lewis, was brought up speaking Gaelic and English. He studied at the universities of Aberdeen, Cambridge and Wales (Bangor). He is Professor of Celtic at Glasgow University. Founder and Editor of the Gaelic quarterly *Gairm* since 1952, he is the author of many academic works. His collected poems in Gaelic, *Creachadh na Clàrsaich (Plundering the Harp)*, was published in 1982.

An Tobar

Tha tobar beag am meadhon a' bhaile
's am feur ga fhalach,
am feur gorm sùghor ga dhlùth thughadh,
fhuair mi brath air bho sheann chaillich,
ach thuirt i, "Tha 'm frith-rathad fo raineach
far am minig a choisich mi le'm chogan,
's tha'n cogan fhèin air dèabhadh."
Nuair sheall mi 'na h-aodann preasach
chunnaic mi 'n raineach a' fàs mu thobar a sùilean
's ga fhalach bho shireadh 's bho rùintean,
's ga dhùnadh 's ga dhùnadh.

"Cha teid duine an diugh don tobar tha sin"
thuirt a' chailleach, "mar a chaidh sinne
nuair a bha sinn òg,
ged tha 'm bùrn ann cho brèagh 's cho geal."

'S nuair sheall mi troimhn raineach 'na sùilean
chunnaic mi lainnir a' bhùirn ud
a ni slàn gach ciùrradh
gu ruig ciùrradh cridhe.

"Is feuch an tadhail thu dhòmhsa,"
thuirt a' chailleach, "ga b'ann le meòirean,
's thoir thugam boinne den uisge chruaidh sin
a bheir rudhadh gu m' ghruaidhean."
Lorg mi an tobar air èiginn
's ged nach b'ise bu mhotha feum air
'sann thuice a thug mi 'n eudail.

Dh' fhaodadh nach eil anns an tobar
ach nì a chunnaic mi 'm bruadar,
oir nuair chaidh mi an diugh ga shireadh
cha d'fhuair mi ach raineach is luachair,
's tha sùilean na caillich dùinte
's tha lì air tighinn air an luathghair.

The Well

Right in the village there's a little well
and the grass hides it,
green grass in sap closely thatching it.
I heard of it from an old woman
but she said: "The path is overgrown with bracken
where I often walked wih my cogie,
and the cogie itself is warped."
When I looked in her lined face
I saw the bracken growing round the well of her eyes,
and hiding it from seeking and from desires,
and closing it, closing it.

"Nobody goes to that well now,"
said the old woman, "as we once went,
when we were young,
though its water is lovely and white."
And when I looked in her eyes through the bracken
I saw the sparkle of that water
that makes whole every hurt
till the hurt of the heart.

"And will you go there for me,"
said the old woman, "even with a thimble,
and bring me a drop of that hard water
that will bring colour to my cheeks."
I found the well at last,
and though her need was not the greatest
it was to her I brought the treasure.

It may be that the well
is something I saw in a dream,
for today when I went to seek it
I found only bracken and rushes,
and the old woman's eyes are closed
and a film has come over their merriment.

Achadh-Bhuana

Air feasgar meallta a-measg nan adag,
is pàirt gun a bhuain, thàinig tu 'n rathad,
is chuir mi mo speal an sin am falach
air eagal gun dèanadh am faobhar do ghearradh.

Bha ar saoghal cho cruinn ris an achadh-bhuana
ged bha cuid dheth abaich is cuid dheth uaine,
an là ri obair 's an oidhch' ri bruadar,
is dh'èirich a' ghealach a meadhon suaimhneis.

Dh'fhàg mi beagan ri bhuain a-màireach
is choisich sinn còmhla eadar na ràthan,
thuit thu air speal bha fear eile air fhàgail,
is ghearradh do chneas, is dhiùlt e slànadh.

Harvest Field

One deceptive evening, among the sheaves, with some of the corn uncut, you came by,
and I put my scythe then in hiding, for fear that the edge of the blade would cut you.
    Our world was rounded like the harvest field, though a part was ripe and a part green,
the day to work and the night to dream, and the moon rose in the midst of content.
    I left a little to cut on the morrow, and we walked together between the swathes: you
fell on a scythe that another had left, and your skin was cut, and refused healing.

Clann-Nighean an Sgadain

An gàire mar chraiteachan salainn
ga fhroiseadh bho 'm beul,
an sàl 's am picil air an teanga,
's na miaran cruinne, goirid a dheanadh giullachd,
no a thogadh leanabh gu socair, cuimir,
seasgair, fallain,
gun mhearachd,
's na sùilean cho domhainn ri fèath.

B'e bun-os-cionn na h-eachdraidh a dh' fhàg iad
'nan tràillean aig ciùrairean cutach,
thall 's a-bhos air Galldachd 's an Sasainn.
Bu shaillte an duais a thàrr iad
ás na mìltean bharaillean ud,
gaoth na mara geur air an craiceann,
is eallach a' bhochdainn 'nan ciste,
is mara b'e an gàire
shaoileadh tu gu robh an teud briste.

Ach bha craiteachan uaille air an cridhe,
ga chumail fallain,
is bheireadh cutag an teanga
slisinn á fanaid nan Gall —
agus bha obair rompa fhathast
nuair gheibheadh iad dhachaigh,
ged nach biodh maoin ac':
air oidhche robach gheamhraidh,
ma bha siud an dàn dhaibh,
dheanadh iad daoine.

The Herring Girls

Their laughter like a sprinkling of salt
showered from their lips,
brine and pickle on their tongues,
and the stubby short fingers that could handle fish,
or lift a child gently, neatly,
safely, wholesomely,
unerringly,
and the eyes that were as deep as a calm.

The topsy-turvy of history had made them
slaves to short-arsed curers,
here and there in the Lowlands, in England.
Salt the reward they won
from those thousands of barrels,
the sea-wind sharp on their skins,
and the burden of poverty in their kists,
and were it not for their laughter
you might think the harp-string was broken.

But there was a sprinkling of pride on their hearts,
keeping them sound,
and their tongues' gutting-knife
would tear a strip from the Lowlanders' mockery —
and there was work awaiting them
when they got home,
though they had no wealth:
on a wild winter's night,
if that were their lot,
they would make men.

Srath Nabhair

Anns an adhar dhubh-ghorm ud,
àirde na sìorraidheachd os ar cionn,
bha rionnag a' priobadh ruinn
's i freagairt mireadh an teine
ann an cabair taigh m' athar
a' bhlianna thugh sinn an taigh le bleideagan sneachda.

Agus siud a' bhlianna cuideachd
a shlaod iad a' chailleach don t-sitig,
a shealltainn cho eòlach 's a bha iad air an Fhìrinn,
oir bha nid aig eunlaith an adhair
(agus cròthan aig na caoraich)
ged nach robh àit aice-se anns an cuireadh i a ceann fòidhpe.

A Shrath Nabhair 's a Shrath Chill Donnain,
is beag an t-iongnadh ged a chinneadh am fraoch àlainn oirbh,
a' falach nan lotan a dh' fhàg Pàdraig Sellar 's a sheòrsa,
mar a chunnaic mi uair is uair boireannach cràbhaidh
a dh' fhiosraich dòrainn an t-saoghail-sa
is sìth Dhè 'na sùilean.

Strathnaver

In that blue-black sky,
as high above us as eternity,
a star was winking at us,
answering the leaping flames of fire
in the rafters of my father's house,
that year we thatched the house with snowflakes.

And that too was the year
they hauled the old woman out on to the dung-heap,
to demonstrate how knowledgeable they were in Scripture,
for the birds of the air had nests
(and the sheep had folds)
though she had no place in which to lay down her head.

O Strathnaver and Strath of Kildonan,
it is little wonder that the heather should bloom on your slopes,
hiding the wounds that Patrick Sellar, and such as he, made,
just as time and time again I have seen a pious woman
who has suffered the sorrow of this world,
with the peace of God shining from her eyes.

Cruaidh?

Cuil-lodair, is Briseadh na h-Eaglaise,
is briseadh nan tacannan —
lamhachas-làidir dà thrian de ar comas;
'se seòltachd tha dhìth oirnn.
Nuair a theirgeas a' chruaidh air faobhar na speala
caith bhuat a' chlach-lìomhaidh;
chan eil agad ach iarann bog
mur eil de chruas nad innleachd na ni sgathadh.

Is caith bhuat briathran mìne
oir chan fhada bhios briathran agad;
tha Tuatha Dè Danann fon talamh,
tha Tìr nan Og anns an Fhraing,
's nuair a ruigeas tu Tìr a' Gheallaidh,
mura bi thu air t' aire,
coinnichidh Sasannach riut is plìon air,
a dh' innse dhut gun tug Dia, bràthair athar, còir dha anns an fhearann.

Steel?

Culloden, the Disruption,
and the breaking up of the tack-farms* —   * leased farms
two thirds of our power is violence;
it is cunning we need.
When the tempered steel near the edge of the scythe-blade is worn
throw away the whetstone;
you have nothing left but soft iron
unless your intellect has a steel edge that will cut clean.

And throw away soft words,
for soon you will have no words left;
the Tuatha Dè Danann are underground,
the Land of the Ever-young is in France,
and when you reach the Promised Land,
unless you are on your toes,
a bland Englishman will meet you,
and say to you that God, his uncle, has given him a title to the land.

Note: Tuatha Dè Danann, a supernatural race in Ireland, sometimes said to be the progenitors of
the fairies.

Cisteachan-Laighe

Duin' àrd, tana
's fiasag bheag air,
's locair 'na làimh:
gach uair theid mi seachad
air bùth-shaoirsneachd sa' bhaile,
's a thig gu mo chuinnlean fàileadh na min-sàibh,
thig gu mo chuimhne cuimhne an àit ud,
le na cisteachan-laighe,
na h-ùird 's na tairgean,
na sàibh 's na sgeilbean,
is mo sheanair crom,
is sliseag bho shliseag ga locradh
bhon bhòrd thana lom.

Mus robh fhios agam dè bh' ann bàs;
beachd, bloigh fios, boillsgeadh
den dorchadas, fathann den t-sàmhchair.
'S nuair a sheas mi aig uaigh,
là fuar Earraich, cha dainig smuain

thugam air na cisteachan-laighe
a rinn esan do chàch:
'sann a bha mi 'g iarraidh dhachaigh,
far am biodh còmhradh, is tea, is blàths.

Is anns an sgoil eile cuideachd,
san robh saoir na h-inntinn a' locradh,
cha tug mi 'n aire do na cisteachan-laighe,
ged a bha iad 'nan suidhe mun cuairt orm;
cha do dh' aithnich mi 'm brèid Beurla,
an lìomh Gallda bha dol air an fhiodh,
cha do leugh mi na facail air a' phràis,
cha do thuig mi gu robh mo chinneadh a' dol bàs.
Gus an dainig gaoth fhuar an Earraich-sa
a locradh a' chridhe;
gus na dh' fhairich mi na tairgean a' dol tromham,
's cha shlànaich tea no còmhradh an cràdh.

Coffins

A tall thin man
with a short beard,
and a plane in his hand:
whenever I pass
a joiner's shop in the city,
and the scent of sawdust comes to my nostrils,
memories return of that place,
with the coffins,
the hammers and nails,
saws and chisels,
and my grandfather, bent,
planing shavings
from a thin, bare plank.

Before I knew what death was;
or had any notion, a glimmering
of the darkness, a whisper of the stillness.
And when I stood at his grave,
on a cold Spring day, not a thought
came to me of the coffins
he made for others:
I merely wanted home
where there would be talk, and tea, and warmth.

And in the other school also,
where the joiners of the mind were planing,
I never noticed the coffins,
though they were sitting all round me;
I did not recognise the English braid,
the Lowland varnish being applied to the wood,
I did not read the words on the brass,
I did not understand that my race was dying
Until the cold wind of this Spring came
to plane the heart;
until I felt the nails piercing me,
and neither tea nor talk will heal the pain.

Am Bodach-Ròcais

An oidhch' ud
thàinig am bodach-ròcais dhan taigh-chèilidh:
fear caol àrd dubh
is aodach dubh air.
Shuidh e air an t-sèis
is thuit na cairtean ás ar làmhan.
Bha fear a siud
ag innse sgeulachd air Conall Gulban
is reodh na faclan air a bhilean.
Bha boireannach 'na suidh' air stòl
ag òran, 's thug e 'n toradh ás a' cheòl.
Ach cha do dh'fhàg e falamh sinn:
thug e òran nuadh dhuinn,
is sgeulachdan na h-àird an Ear,
is sprùilleach de dh'fheallsanachd Geneva,
is sguab e 'n teine á meadhon an làir
's chuir e 'n tùrlach loisgeach nar broillichean.

Scarecrow

That night
the scarecrow came into the cèilidh-house:
a tall, thin black-haired man
wearing black clothes.
He sat on the bench
and the cards fell from our hands.

One man
was telling a folktale about Conall Gulban
and the words froze on his lips.
A woman was sitting on a stool,
singing songs, and he took the goodness out of the music.
But he did not leave us empty-handed:
he gave us a new song,
and tales from the Middle East,
and fragments of the philosophy of Geneva,
and he swept the fire from the centre of the floor
and set a searing bonfire in our breasts.

Cotriona Mhòr

Tha do dhealbh ann an cùl m' inntinn
gun sgleò air,
daingeann, suidhichte
a-measg nan ìomhaighean briste,
a-measg a luasgain,
gun aois a' laigh air ach an aois a bhà thu,
clàr mòr an aodainn mar ghleoc air stad
air madainn Earraich,
gam chur ri uair a' bhaile
leis a' ghliocas sin
nach robh an eisimeil leabhraichean,
leis an àbhachdas, leis a' ghearradh-cainnt
a bha a' leum á cridhe a' chinnidh
mus deach a chèiseadh,
mus deach a valve ùr ann
a chumadh ag obair e anns an t-saoghal ùr.
Siud iuchair mo mhuseum,
an clàr air an cluich mi mo bheul-aithris,
an spaid-bheag leis an dùisg mi fonn
na linne a tha nise seachad,
an ìomhaigh tha cumail smachd air na h-ìomhaighean-brèige.

Cotriona Mhòr

Your picture is at the back of my mind
undimmed,
steady, set
among the broken images,
amid the movements,
untouched by age except the age you were,
the great round of the face like a clock stopped
on a Spring morning,
keeping me to the village time
with that wisdom
that flourished without books,
with the fun, the cleverness-with-words
that leapt from the heart of the race
before it was encased,
before it had the new valve in it
to keep it going in the new world.
That is the key to my museum,
the record on which I play my folklore,
the trowel with which I turn the ground
of the age that is now gone,
the image that keeps control over false images.

"Who are the Scots?"

Thainig fuachd an Earraich
anns na cnàmhan aosda againn,
deàrrsadh anns na cnuibheanan,
beagan de chrith anns na crògan,
's gun fhios carson
thòisich sinn a' bruidhinn air ar n-òige,
air an t-sealg a rinn sinn air an Fhoghar ud,
air a ruidhle dhanns sinn fo ghealach abachaidh an eòrna,
air an aodach mheileabhaid
's air a' ghrèim làidir
roimhn a' ghrèim seo thàinig
a bhreith air sgamhan oirnn.

A' tionndadh nan grìogagan
air an t-seann mheileabhaid
le na làmhan critheanach,
an crù air lapadh
's ar n-uaill anns a' chruan.

"Who are the Scots?"

The Spring cold
penetrated our old bones,
our knuckles reddened
and our hands shook a little,
and not knowing why
we began to talk about our youth,
and the hunting we did that autumn,
the reel we danced beneath the harvest moon,
the velvet cloth
and the hard grip we had
before this pneumonia
gripped our lungs.

Turning the beads
on the old velvet
with shaky hands,
the blood thinning,
taking a pride in enamel.

Ola

Nuair a bha mi beag
bhiodh bodach a' tighinn a bhùth mo sheanar
gach là laghail, a dh'iarraidh botal ola:
fear dhe na h-òighean glice 's dòcha —
cha deidhinn an urras nach e òigh a bh'ann co-dhiù —
a bha cumail sùgh ris an t-siobhaig;
bodach ait, a ghàire faisg air,
ach beagan de dh' eagal air roimhn an dorch.

Tha iad ag ràdh an diugh gu bheil an saoghal-bràth de dh'ol' againn
anns an dùthaich bheag seo —
bhig seo, bhog seo? —
gu bheil sinn air bhog ann a lèig ola.
Tha mi 'n dòchas gu ruig an t-siobhag oirre.

Oil

When I was a boy
an old man used to come to my grandfather's shop
every lawful day, for a bottle of oil:
one of the wise virgins perhaps —
a virgin in any case, I dare say —
who kept the lamp-wick wet;
a jolly old man, ready to laugh,
but a little afraid of the dark.

They say now that we have an eternity of oil
in this little land —
this toty, flabby land? —
that we are afloat on a lake of oil.
I hope the wick can reach it.

Fòghnan na h-Alba

Tha am fòghnan a' fàs ann a leas,
ùir dhubh mun cuairt air,
air a dheagh ghabhail uime,
an ùir air a glanadh,
ri thaobh, feur na faiche
air a bhearradh gu cuimir;
's e fhèin 'na sheasamh ann a sin
'na aodach-Sàbaid, cho grinn,
speiseanta, dìreach,
gun lùbadh a-null no nall,
gun dragh ga chur air flùraichean eile,
na frioghanan beaga cho modhail,
mar gum b'e 'n H.L.I. air parade.
Cha robh dùil 'am ri boladh làidir
bho fhlùr fòghnain, ach chaidh mi null
a dh'fhaighneachd, mar gum b'ann,
is chrom mi mo cheann,
is bhuail 'na mo chuinnlean
fàileadh *Old Spice.*

Ach tha mi mionnaichte
gu bheil fòghnanan fhathast a' fàs
a-measg chreagan,
is fàileadh na gaoithe dhiubh.
Tha mi dol air an tòir.

Thistle of Scotland

The thistle grows in a garden,
black loam around it,
well cared for,
the soil weeded,
beside it the lawn grass
neatly cut;
and it standing there
in its Sunday clothes, so neat,
tidy, erect,
bending neither this way nor that,
not annoying other flowers,
the little prickles as polite
as the H.L.I.* on parade.   * Highland Light Infantry
I did not expect a strong scent
from a thistle flower, but went over
to enquire, as it were,
and bent my head,
and there impinged on my nostrils
the scent of *Old Spice*.

But I could swear
there are still thistles growing
among rocks,
with the scent of the wind off them.
I am going to look for them.

Alastair Mackie

Alastair Mackie, the foremost poet writing to-day in the Scottish north-east dialect, has been undeservedly neglected.

A lad o' pairts, brought up in working-class Aberdeen, he was inspired to write in Scots by the example of Hugh MacDiarmid. He takes his poetic role seriously (though not pompously) seeing himself as a latter-day Ulysses engaged in a poetic voyage of discovery, hence the title of his latest collection 'Back-green Odyssey'.

He has translated expertly from French, Italian and Russian, finding Scots a most appropriate medium. His craftsmanship is obvious in his deft handling of various verse forms. Although his poems are generally serious there is a delightful infusion in his work of wit and humour. In 'Scots Pegasus' he is pessimistic about the future of Scots doric poetry, but assuredly Alastair Mackie 'kens the horseman's word'.

Through the blur of hindsight I offer this paradox: chance caused me to be a Scots poet. In 1954 I taught English at Stromness Academy and in that year George Mackay Brown lent me a rare copy of *Sangschaw*, a seminal cluster of lyrics by the late Hugh MacDiarmid. The experience of digesting this key work, indispensable for the understanding of modern Scots poetry, was like absorbing a mind-bending chemical.

It was the Scots words; 'the haill clanjamfrie', 'i the howe-dumb-deid o the cauld hairst nicht', 'thae trashy bleezin French-like folk', their unfamiliarity, their onomatopoetic vigour, their 'otherness', married to a lyric assurance that reached down and tapped for me a layer of Scots not entirely overlaid by formal education.

I was brought up in a working-class household where Scots was the medium, and in a street where it was the accepted norm by my peers of both sexes. My first attempts were, naturally, apprentice work, tentatively exploring my resources. But it soon became apparent that I had to extend the word-hoard. I became an archaeologist. I pored over an old Scots dictionary alighting on words that I didn't know I knew and others that fascinated me by their obsoleteness, and more importantly, their potential as buried deposits that could be pressed into the service of poetry. It was a matter of choice and chance. My Scots is eclectic, though I build from a north-east found. For my purposes, that any given word is obsolete, is immaterial. Of capital importance is its placement in the poetic context in such a way that it produces the paradoxical effect of being at once alien and irreplaceable, creating that surprise factor that is one of the ingredients of poetry.

From the beginning I also began to translate pieces from the French, the foreign language I know best. This venture was motivated by the need to discover whether Scots, if it were a viable medium in itself, could cope with the traditional complexities of translation. Over the years this exploration extended to embrace Italian, German and Russian.

My living-room window confronts a horizon of sea, as it did in Orkney. This symbol of space links up with my endeavour to extend the scope of Scots poetry as far as it was given to accomplish. Finally, it is not by chance that my hero is Odysseus.

Born and educated in Aberdeen, passing through Skene Square Primary, Robert Gordon's College, and after war service, graduated in English Honours at Aberdeen University. In 1951 took up a post in Stromness Academy and from there went to Waid Academy in Anstruther. In 1983 took premature retirement 'to escape the hit men of Munn and Dunning'. Now copes with a new situation and 'the intolerable wrestle with words'.

Pieta

Her face was thrawed*.   * contorted
She wisna aa come*.   * in her right mind

In her spurtle-shankit* airms   * porridge stick
the wummin held oot her first bairn.
It micht hae been a mercat day
and him for sale.
Naebody stoppit to niffer*.   * haggle

His life bleed cled his briest
wi a new reid semmit*.   * undervest
He'd hippens* for deid claes.   * napkins

Aifter the boombers* cleck†   * bombers; † dropping
and the sodgers traik* thro the skau†   * trudge; † devastation
there's an auld air sterts up —
bubblin and greetin.
It's a ballant* mithers sing   * ballad
on their hunkers* i the stour†   * heels; † dust
for a bairn deid.
They ken it by hert.

It's the cauldest grue* i the universe   * shudder
yon skelloch*.   * screech
It never waukens the deid.

In Absentia

"We've no heard fae God this while,"
said ane o the angels.
It was at a synod
o the metaphors.

Cam a wind;
it was aabody speirin*   * inquiring
"Wha?"
into themsels.

It was heard by the sauls
o Baudelaire and Pascal.
They fell thro the muckle hole
Whaur the question gantit*   * yawned

In the boddom* Jesus sweatit   * bottom
"Consummatum est."
And Nietzsche
hou he laucht and laucht.

The maist o fowk bein neither
philosophers or theologians
kept gaun* to the kirk.
Whiles, like*.

* going
* from time to time

Syne God said: "Noo I'm awa,
mak a kirk or a mill o't."

And God gaed to the back o beyond
i the midst o aathing.

New Moon

Heuch* edge o ice;
the fremmit* rim o a Mongol shield
i the smorin* steppes o space

* sickle
* alien
* choking

kyths*.

* takes shape

Asia's ahint*, It's Europe's shot
this snell* gloamin-faa†.

* behind
* sharply cold; † evening twilight

Nether* lip,
the face o ye mirklins*
there's an eerie lauch at the wicks o your mou*.
Is't your first kill?

* lower
* darkens
* corners of your mouth

Finger nail whitens
amon aa that air's blue bleed.
The grip o the sliver*!

* slice

And syne the starns*.
The birstle* o their schiltrons†.

* stars
* bristle; † spearheads

The menace o hemmert* bress ower the sea.
The sun is smiddyin* a targe.

* hammered
* forging

It bydes* a month for bleed.

* waits

Adolescence

Gin* they wid leave me alane!   * if only

Whit ails me
I dinna ken.

Look ahint* my een, ye'll fin   * behind
het* saut† and love-stounds‡.   * hot; † salt; ‡ love pangs

Thae days it cams easy
like — dinna greet* lassie —   * weep

A beast mum and tethert
to a stound*.   * throbbing ache

The soond o the guitars
and me dwaumin* thro them.   * daydreaming

And did he nae smile to me?
But he did smile to me!

The keekin-gless* is my frien   * mirror
I tell it aathing jist lookin.

It says naething the haill time
but — ye're bonny quine* —   * lass

I fill up its laneliness
wi my ain dowie* face   * sad

and when my een crack
it shares my hert-brak,

cut gless lookin at cut gless.

Mongol Quine

Elbucks* on the herbour waa
the mongol quine*
collogues*
wi hersel.

* elbows
* girl
* converses

Her blond baa-heid* wags
frae side to side.
Noo she's a wag-at-the-wa*
noo a croon.

* roundhead
* pendulum clock

Wha said grace and grouwin*
to this mistak?
A ban* was on her
fae further back.

* blessing or christening
* curse

Nievie* nievie nack nack
whit hand'll ye tak tak?
She got the wrang hand
and didna pan oot*.

* fist
* work out well

She's got pig's een,
a bannock face,
and hurdies* that rowed†
like twa muckle bools.

* buttocks; † rolled

She wints for naething. Yet
she's singin till the distance.
Ayont* the hert-brak, her een
are set for ever on an unkent airt*.

* beyond
* direction

Mind on the Nichts?

(*Remember the nights*)

Ye said; 'When we're auld
wull ye mind on the nichts, my dear
wull ye mind on the nichts?'

Oh aye,
easy when the veins buller*   * surge
as they did jist nou,
nae when we're winnlestraes*.   * withered straws

Easy when ye ken ye can, mair or less,
nae when ye canna, ever.

It's a kittle* pint†. I'd nae be leal‡ to ye   * nice; † point; ‡ loyal
gin* I were to say 'Aye' ootricht.   * if

Wummin, the body's a begeck*,   * disappointment
ye're rigged oot to be jiltit.

There's craw-feet ablow your een* nou.   * eyes
They'll howk* aa ower your face.   * dig

Wait till ablow* the sheets   * below
there's nocht but twa crawsticks.

Wait till there's dotterin* and pechin†   * staggering; † panting
and oor bodies twa guffs*.   * smells

Forby* ye ken fine   * also
love weers* oot as mony nicht gouns.   * wears
We micht be cleedin* a corpse.   * clothing

Still, I had hopes tho.
Like I hope I can haud that lang cleuk*   * claw, hook
that ran ower me like watter
and say to the neebrin mirk* —   * darkness

'Ye fushionless* anatomy, aye, I mind.'   * feeble
And I'll listen thro your loof*   * palm of hand
for the far-aff brack o your bleed
when ye rizz* to me and syne† fell fae me,   * rose; † then
sleepin soond nou.
And the nicht still young.

Scots Pegasus

Oor Scots Pegasus
is a timmer* naig†
wi a humphy* back and cockle een†.

* wooden; † horse
* hump; † cockeyes

He ettles* to flee
but his intimmers* are fu o the deid-chack†.
Gin* he rins ava†
he pechs* sair.
And skelbs* drap aff like sharn†.

* attempts
* guts; † woodworm noises
* if; † at all
* pants
* splinters; † dung

He's fed on bruck*
scranned* fae aa the airts.
This gies him the belly-thraw*
and yon etten and spewed* look.

* scraps
* scavenged
* belly-ache
* pasty, unhealthy

Makars* whiles
fling a leg ower his rig-bane*
and crank the hunnle on his spauld*.

* poets
* back
* shoulderbone

He taks a turn roon the park
but never gets aff the grun*
or oot o the bit.
This mishanter's* caad
in some stables —
'A new voice in Lallans'.

* ground

* misadventure

Ithers, brither Scots
gie him the hee-haw*.

* laugh him to scorn

The hert o the nut is this* —
naebody, dammt, kens the horseman's word*.

* the essential point
* secret word handed down by horseman

Backgreen Odyssey

Sonnet No. 1

The sun's oot. I sit, my pipe alunt*, and puff.   ** glowing*
The claes-line's pegged wi washin. They could be
sails. (Let them) Hou they rax* and thraw†, and yet   ** strain; † twist*
caa* naething forrit†. Gress grouws on my deck.   ** drive; † forward*

Thro the wheepcracks o my sails the blue
wine o the sea is blinkin to the bouwl rim
o the horizon whaur my classic tap
the Berwick Law hides oor nothrin* Athens.   ** northern*

Nae watters for an Odyssey ye'll think
whaur jist tankers, coasters, seine-netters ply.
Still, ablow this blue roof and burst o sun

my mind moves amon islands. Ulysses-
dominie, I cast aff the tether-tow*   ** mooring rope*
and steer my boat sittin on my doup-end*.   ** backside*

Backgreen Odyssey

Sonnet No. 5

My main deck is a green*. Near the foreheid†   ** drying green; † prow*
the kitchen plot. I am weel stockit wi
vittles. On the starboard gunwales, flooers
and bushes whaur the birds scutter* and pleep†.   ** scurry; † cries*

I sit here, the captain and the haill* crew   ** entire*
and keep my sun-birsled* watches dwaumin†.   ** sunburnt; † daydreaming*
Whiles I scour the sky-line, whiles I scrieve* drauchts   ** write*
in the log-book o my tethert vaigin*;   ** voyaging*

the sea's a ticht blue swatch*; a thin skraichin†   ** pattern; † yelling*
o bairns rises fae the beach; a sea gull
peenges* like a wean and oars the air back.   ** whines*

I canna read my Homer in this sun.
I feel the reid meat o my body fry.
My Odyssey is jist a doverin*.

* nodding off

Backgreen Odyssey

Sonnet No. 13

Streekit* oot ahint† the winbreak I let
Homer drap. The print jobs my een*. Instead
I watch a sma green-like beastie craalin
ower the blindrift o sunsheen on the page.

* stretched out; † behind
* eyes

It sang o him blattered* by Poseidon
ower the mirk* wineskin o the sea. I watcht
this sudden drappin fae the air on till
the hexameters. Whaur was his Ithaca?

* windtorn
* dark

I felt like the yird-shakker* himsel then
heich* abeen† this nochtie‡ o a craitur.
I let him streetch his pins a bit. A god

* earth-shaker
* high; † above; ‡ non-entity

can byde his time and wyle* it tae, whit's mair.
Atween ennui and yokey fingers
I skytit* him aff the page. Yaawned syne.

* choose
* swatted

Hoose

A granite ship oor hoose,
granite sky-lines shouthert* the fower airts.
The bows grew tatties, cabbages and neeps*;
a dryin green and wash-hoose at the starn*.
On the main deck tiger lilies blew orange tooteroos,
and dusty millers, a fine stew on their lips,
and butter-baas happit* up like presents.
Forrit touzle-heidit asters shook,
the black currants' pit-mark worlds.
Fae the gunwales privet hedges sprootit*.

* shouldered
* turnips
* stern

* dressed, clad

* sprouted

My granny sailed on't, my spinster aunt,
forby* the six o us,   * also
echt* thegither in fower cabins.   * eight

The elements in their seasons shoggit* it,   * jostled
but we weathert aathing . . . birth, death,
broken time, disease . . . We never foonert*.   * foundered

Fae the iron railin ye could look ower
and watch the freethe* and stillness o the sea.   * freedom

I was a neb-in-the-book* Odysseus,   * nose-in-the book
a dwaumy* spinnly bide-at-hame†,   * dreamy; † stay-at-home
tethert for years to the quay-side o the street.

The kitchen was oor nicht school
faur* we hunched ower lessons,   * where
my three sisters and mysel. The room's gear*   * furniture
I mind, was solid stuff, shiftit roon whiles
but the table held the middle o the fleer*,   * floor
a fower-legged god to bakin and to lear*.   * learning

The gas mantle's yalla* star biled and bizzit   * yellow
abeen my father's black heid deep
in the pre-war 'Evening Express' —
Lindberg, Dolfuss, Abyssinia . . . Wullie Mills.
Mither darned or knittit, or in a note-book
warstled* wi the sma cheenge o a blocker's pey,   * wrestled
the insurance, the menadge*, the coal accoont . . .   * pre-war thrift club
But me the clever een, I was at the sums,
parsin, makkin maps . . .

It was a sma bit faimly world
fed and cled on a quarryman's steeny* wage.   * stony
And the white ceilin streetcht its moose-wabby* tent   * cobwebbed
abeen* oor heids.   * above
          We said oor prayers in bed
and fell asleep. God's job it was to keep us
happit fae aa hairm and gin we never
waukent, oor souls wid be safe richt enough
in his auld man's hands.

Primary Teachers

My primary teachers o the Thirties
maun* aa be middle-aged skeletons by nou,   * must
Aa weemin they were.
       The early snaw in their hair.
They pit up wi impetigo, flechy* heids,   * lousy
and bairns that couldna pey their books —
       the fathers were on the broo*   * unemployed
And yet they did learn us, yon auld wives,
We chantit tables like bairn-rhymes
to keep aff the inspectors or the heidie*.   * headmaster
And when we spelled the classroom skriechit*   * screeched
sclatey* music fae oor soap-scoured slates.   * slaty
Their scuds* were murder — the Lochgelly soond.   * leather straps
'Don't turn on the water-works' they girned.
       (They spoke English)
They kent naething o new methods
but in their fashion they were as teuch*   * tough
as gauleiters, ramrods withoot breists.
They did their T.C.'s* prood.   * training colleges
       I salute ye nou,
Miss Smith, Miss Tough, Miss McIvor —
steam-hemmers somebody maun hae loved.

Bigamist

Poetry's my second wife.
For oors*   * hours
I sit wi her ben the room.
I hiv to listen;
she's got a good Scots tongue in her heid.

Oor merraige is a lang scuttery* tyauve†   * fussy; † struggle
on white sheets. Sometimes
she winna come ava. I'm fair deaved*   * deafened
wi the soonless claik* o her.   * gossip
"Listen to this," she'll sough* for the umpteenth time.   * whisper

The next minute (or day) it's "Na;
na, I didna mean that ye see.
Whit I mint was . . ."
God damnt, wumman,
my heid's bizzin.
I canna come speed* wi my wark.   * progress

And you?
Ye'll be knittin mebbe,
finger nebs like fechtin spiders,
you and your sprauchle o twa quines*,   * lasses
glowerin at the TV.
My exilt faimly in the livin room.

And me?
I'm cairryin on wi anither quine;
a limmer*, a jaud†, a   * loose woman; † thrawn female
bletherin bitch.
When your heid keeks roon the door
and ye say, "Suppertime"
ye gie a bit sklent* at the sheets   * glance
whaur she's lyin, and I see on your mou*   * mouth
a bit smile, jist that bit look
that says:
        MY shot* nou.   * turn

Burns Singer

Burns Singer, born in 1928 and died in 1964, was probably the greatest single loss Scottish poetry has suffered this century. A rootless cosmopolitan, his poetry at times has an extraordinary strangeness so that it seems in MacDiarmid's words to be coming from 'outer space': but he was perhaps, apart from MacDiarmid himself, the most ambitious of the Scottish poets of this century, the most intensely absorbed in his art, as well as in speculations on a wide range of ideas in modern thought. His training in science — he worked for a time in the Marine Laboratory in Aberdeen — uniquely equipped him to be a writer of modern sensibility: he was also greatly interested in philosophical speculations on language such as those which were carried out by Wittgenstein. In poetry he was influenced by Dylan Thomas, George Barker, and most especially W. S. Graham with whom he shares an obsession with the limits of communication.

His life was a tragic one: his father was a failed salesman, his mother committed suicide. He lived at times in Glasgow, Aberdeen, London and Cambridge. He was born in New York. His marriage to an American psychologist brought him perhaps the most sustained happiness he had known.

In the selection here we have tried to show his work at its most comprehensible; his later work tended to become increasingly abstract. However, in some of these poems, we find a lyric quality and a handling of language which are absolutely unique. His voice was at times unmistakably his own, and unlike anybody else's, and his love poems in particular have an individual blend of exhilaration and recognition of love's limits. His mastery of metaphor was complete. For those who wish to explore his work further the whole poem *The Transparent Prisoner* is of great interest, as is his masterly *Marcus Antoninus*, an examination of power and action, which is too long to be included here. To open the collection *Still and All*, Singer wrote:

TO THE CRITIC

I have refrained
From trying to find
A law and order in poetry.
If you want rules
And styles and schools
Apply to the nearest côtery.

and

STILL AND ALL (extract)

I give my word on it. There is no way
Other than this. There is no other way
Of speaking. I am my name. I find my place
Empty without a word, and my word is
Given again. It is nothing less than all
Given away again, and all still truly
Returned on a belief. Believe me now.
There is no other. There is no other way.

These words run vertical in their slim green tunnels
Without any turning away. They turn into
The first flower and speak from a silent bell.
But underneath it is as always still
Truly awakening, slowly and slowly turning
About a shadow scribbled down by sunlight
And turning about my name. I am in my
Survival's hands. I am my shadow's theme.

A Letter

Tonight I'll meet you: yes, tonight. I know
There are, perhaps, a thousand miles — but not
Tonight. Tonight I go inside. I take
All the walls down, the bric-à-brac, the trash,
The tawdry pungent dust these months have gathered
Into a heap about me. I must prepare
And somehow move away from the slow world,

The circling menace with its throat and teeth
Attempting definition; and brush off
Those thoughts that, clinging like thin fallen hairs,
Make me unclean: for I must go tonight
And, secret from my shadow, go alone
Back to the hour when you yourself became
So much my own that even my own eyes
Seemed strange compared to you who were a new
Complete pervasive organ of all sense
Through which I saw and heard and more than touched
The very dignity of experience.

The Brush-off

You pass politely away
Back among the shrill pygmies.
Their bare faces project
Like clocks about me.

This one has a name.
It hurries up to me.
While that one gives away
All I have wasted.

The clocks are very kind.
Each in its narrow circle
Charmingly reflects
Empty precision.

And each one in return
Asks nothing more of me
Than to represent
A life that's mine.

I watch their flat pale faces
And the black numerals
Till you, my chequered darling,
Disappear inside.

Sunlight

It was a dream in night,
The pier all ropes, a road,
Houses, tiles a-tilting,
Where only sunlight stood.

My bus was made of bridges,
Words I had overheard,
Small streets and talking cages,
Shells that secreted a bird.

It was the South of France.
I climbed the high-built bus
In a sparse but limitless landscape
I knew I could not pass.

So I reversed the corner.
I did not turn. I jumped.
And down on me hard and heavy
Mountains of sunlight were dumped,

With an English pub in the centre
Where wines were cold and dry
And I could feel that sunlight's
Smooth intensity.

Therefore farewell, my lovely;
It was towards you I went
When into dreams at midnight
Summer sunlight bent.

Words Made of Water

Men meet and part;
But meeting men today
I find them frightened,
Frightened and insolent,
Distrustful as myself.

We turn arrogantly toward one another,
Caged in dogmatical dazzle.
Our eyes shine like thin torchlight.
Conflicting truths, we dazzle one another.
Never lately have I known men meet
With only darkness, quite anonymous,
Perched up between them on a song no bird
Would answer for in sunlight.
I have watched carefully but never once
Have I seen the little heaps,
The co-ordinated fragments of muscle, brain, bone,
Creep steadfastly as ants across the planet,
Quite lost in their own excess of contraries,
Make signals, ask for answers,
Humbly and heavily from those they know
Are equally ignorant.

Looking about the streets I find the answers,
Thin blobs of light, enamelled price-lists, brawling,
An impatient competition
Between all those who all know all the answers.

I find also certain bits of paper,
Matchsticks, sodden or cracked or still with safety heads,
Cigarette douts and their empty packets,
And also water,
Water that is stagnant
Or water flowing slowly down the gutter.

I sometimes think that dead men live in water,
That their ghosts inhabit the stagnant puddles,
Their barges float with the gutter water
That they are waiting patiently as water
Until the world is redeemed by doubt,
By each man's love for all those different answers
Dead men have dropped on sundry bits of paper,
From glances blue as smoke, now quite extinguished.

My womenfolk find these thoughts troubling.
Action becomes impossible: choice is impossible
To those who think such things.
On thoughts like these no man ever grew fat.

From: The Transparent Prisoner

Any conditions continued long enough
Will stretch themselves until a man can live
All of him, in them; and the lowest life
Give highest impulse headroom, though he have
A hutch, a hole, a hill, to habit, and
Squalor alone to love and understand.

That is what baffles tyrants. Only death
Can end man's freedom to be all man can.
Prisons are perches. I went underneath
Then came up with a precious undertone
That swirled to song out of the damp dark
Through coughs that came with it and made it stark.

There were enough of them — incarnadined
The shining rock-face with thick frothy spittle,
And hours enough after the coal was mined
To watch how others bended or turned brittle,
Broke in a moment, and the hysteric calm
After the black barred ambulance had come.

Yet in the tunnel, at the rock-face, when
Accumulated by exhaustion, thoughts
Would form and fold and hold themselves close in
About the point of peace, were other states.
The shift, twelve hours had gone, and six more yet.
The pick-axe slithered in my hand like sweat.

Huge blocks and boulders mined off hours ago
Would seem a sick weight, and my stomach turned
Into a sob, and memories of snow
And footprints tapering backwards through it burned,
Like tiny monosyllables blaze, with fear.
My weak arms worked. I seemed to disappear.

Lying along my belly, the rock roof
Two feet above, the wet rock floor upon
My muscles sliding, I seemed to grow aloof
From my own body or to grow a skin,
Flesh, form, and senses, deep within my own
And to retire to live in them alone.

My hands against the coal would grow transparent,
Then, like a match felt softly by its flame,
My arms would char into a wandering current;
Warm radiance crept up them till the same
Vivid transparence flooded every part
And I could see the beating of my heart.

As sedentary worms that burrow in
A froth of sand cement it with a slime
Out of their own skin, I too shed my shine
On to the rock below me till in time
It took the same transparence as myself:
I saw its seed, its kernel, through the filth.

And then above, the rock like catching fire
Bled into clearness to the pointed grass
That bled beyond it; and the sun that higher
Winds in its web this planetary mass
Grew clear; stars stood above it, and ranged behind
Its brightness like the workings of a mind.

I saw the moments and the seasons swim
Precisely through me and I saw them show
Huts, hills and homes, and distance, and my dream
Of little footsteps shrieking in the snow
As they tip into darkness, all grow bright
And smother everything in transparent light.

I watched. A tender clarity became
That moment mine, as clear as through a hand
Bones shadow out into a candle's flame
And tender-terrible as to understand
Faults that the finding of has often killed
Pity and pain in you, fault-ridden child.

And I acknowledged. O I don't know what,
But greater grace than my acknowledgement
Could ever reach the edge of, or forget —
— A tender clarity that would not relent
Till I saw mercy from the merciless brink
Of thoughts which no mind born was born to think:

Poem without a Title

It was so fragile a thing that
Suddenly we were afraid of
What would happen if it
Overtook us; and,
Frightened, we ran.

Then came a new fear that
Perplexed us, because we couldn't
Link fear with the beauty which it
Had brought near us, when,
Frightened, we ran.

We now knew only that
It had seemed terrible (but
Not because we might break it,
Rather it us); so,
Frightened, we ran.

Yet still more terrible that,
It being about to vanish,
Our whole lives should depend on it
Utterly. Therefore,
Frightened, we ran.

Later we learned that
Outside we could find nothing
Which would replace it, nor reach it
Within ourselves, though,
Frightened, we ran.

Peterhead in May

Small lights pirouette
Among these brisk little boats.
A beam, cool as a butler,
Steps from the lighthouse.

Wheelroom windows are dark.
Reflections of light quickly
Skip over them tipsily like
A girl in silk.

One knows there is new paint
And somehow an intense
Suggestion of ornament
Comes into mind.

Imagine elephants here.
They'd settle, clumsily sure
Of themselves and of us and of four
Square meals and of water.

Then you will have it. This
Though a grey and quiet place
Finds nothing much amiss.
It keeps its stillness.

There is no wind. A thin
Mist fumbles above it and,
Doing its best to be gone,
Obscures the position.

This place is quiet or,
Better, impersonal. There
Now you have it. No verdict
Is asked for, no answer.

Yet nets will lie all morning,
Limp like stage scenery,
Unused but significant
Of something to come.

From: Sonnets for a Dying Man

XV

The old man dozed. The hospital quietened.
Nurses went whispering past his unmade bed:
While Mr. Childs, who has no stomach, yawned
And those with papers put them by, unread.
It went all right till tea-time. Then the trays
Trickling like iron water through the ward
Wakened the old man and in prompt relays
The nurses gathered to be reassured.
The old man wakened but to what old tales
Of overwork or underpay or hate
We'll never know. By now it is too late.
But Mr. Childs, who has no stomach, swore
The old man rose and tried to shout before
His eyes went slimy with the look of snails.

XVI

This, I suppose, is what they mean by death,
The senses clogged, the air inhaled upon us:
Your chest is snatched at, torn by your own breath,
While doctors search you for exotic faunas.
Fix the glass slide in flame, stain, and remark
That chain of streptococci under oil.
You look up like a dog that wants to bark
While they transmit your heartbeat through a coil.
Merciful monster, doctor with a serum,
Look at your own eyes in my instrument
And then correct your inferential theorem
About what death is, or rather what you meant.
All you intended was, of course, no lie:
Admit it though, you didn't *mean* to die.

XXIII

Is it perhaps a telephone unanswered,
A sun in trouble, or a star on heat,
The B.B.C. truncating bits of Hansard,
Or is a ghost howling beneath the street?

I do not know what it can be you hear.
I know that you are listening, and I try,
By listening also, not to interfere
With your supreme unshared perplexity.
What words can say to me the words have said
Out there where nothing happens since you are
No longer there for things to happen to
And there's no way of telling what is true
You cannot find me any image for
Our knowledge of our ignorance of the dead.

XLVIII

I promise you by the harsh funeral
Of thought beleaguered in a spun desire,
And by the unlatched hour, and by the fall
Of more than bodies into more than fire:
And by the blackbird with its throat alive,
And by the drowned man with his tongue distended,
By all beginnings never to be ended,
And by an end beyond what we contrive:
I promise you on an authority
Greater, more sure, more hazardous than my own,
Yes, by the sun which suffers in the sky
I promise you — that words of living bone
Will rise out of your grave and kneel beside
A world found dying of the death you died.

To Marie

For Half a Year of Happiness
November 6th: 1956

   For half a year of happiness
    Between us two
   These small barefooted words must run
    Along my pen to you.

They whisper secretly in one
    Another's secret ear:
Heavy black-booted thoughts patrol,
    But cannot hear.

This mob of children from the streets
    Where love is young and we
Playing pavement games, chalk clumsy signs
    And riddle-ree.

O do not be deceived, my dear.
    Sing me a song.
These little gangs, in secret gay,
    Have beaten down those long

Vocabularies, squads of words,
    In sulky navy-blue.
There's half a year of happiness
    Between us two.

Stewart Conn

Stewart Conn, Senior Producer of Drama at the BBC studios in Edinburgh, has developed steadily as a poet of compassion and technical skill. Many of his poems are set in Ayrshire and deal with farmers and farming landscapes with a caring clarity, while others are often about his wife and family, and parents, especially his father. He has been a consistent and generous helper of Scottish writers in his professional role as drama producer, as well as writing a number of fine plays himself.

Among my most vivid memories are those of Harelaw, not far from Kilmarnock where I was brought up. On my father's side the ownership, and before that the tenancy, of this farm went back beyond Burns's day. I recall its byres and rucklifters; ritual new-year shoots; the outlook across the firth, to Ailsa Craig and Arran; its people — and animals. In particular there was my great-uncle Todd with his Clydesdale horses, intensely physical but, through boyhood's eyes, figures of almost mythic proportion.

A persistent seam of poetry has its origin in those Ayrshire days. Passing out of the family the farm came to represent my youth, itself irretrievable. Poems of possession and dispossession are their own attempt at repossession. Above all they are an intended celebration (often, paradoxically, through elegy) of a sturdy breed who belonged to a specific soil as it, for a spell, belonged to them.

Of my subsequent poems, many are set against a changing city backdrop: either the crumbling Victorian sector of Glasgow where I was in fact born, and spent most of my working life; or Edinburgh's east-windy new town, where I now live. They still tend to interweave environment with genealogy, the passage of generations.

These later poems are however far from exclusively urban. Whether responding to a painting itself resonant with feeling (*Kitchen-Maid*) or reflecting on a day's fishing (*End of Season, Drumelzier*), they try to retain and pin down what they can of the vulnerability and fragility of our everyday lives and affections. This in conjunction with their constant awareness of threat, of impending loss, makes them ultimately, I suppose, cries of love and outrage in time's despite.

Stewart Conn was born in Glasgow in 1936, and brought up in Ayrshire. Married with two sons, he now lives in Edinburgh.

Published poetry includes *Thunder in the Air* (Akros, 1967), *The Chinese Tower* (Macdonald, 1967) and three hardback collections, all under Hutchinson's imprint: *Stoats in the Sunlight* (1968), *An Ear to the Ground* (1972: Poetry Book Society Choice) and *Under the Ice* (1978).

Among his published plays are *The King* (Penguin), *The Burning, The Aquarium* and *I Didn't Always Live Here* (John Calder), and *Thistlewood* and *Play Donkey* (Woodhouse Books). Most recently, for television, have been a short film *The Kite* and the screenplay for Neil Gunn's novel *Blood Hunt* (both BBC2).

Harelaw

Ploughlands roll where limekilns lay
    Seeping in craters. Where once dense
    Fibres oozed against gatepost and fence
Till staples burst, firm wheatfields sway:
    And where quarries reeked, intense

With honeysuckle, a truck dumps load
    Upon load of earth, of ash and slag
    For the raking. Spliced hawsers drag
Roots out and wrench the rabbit wood
    Apart as though some cuckoo fugue

Had rioted. On this mossy slope
    That raindrops used to drill and drum
    Through dusk, no nightjar flits nor numb
Hawk hangs as listening foxes lope
    And prowl; no lilac shadows thumb

The heavy air. This holt was mine
   To siege and plunder; here I caged
   Rare beasts or swayed royally on the agèd
Backs of horses — here hacked my secret sign,
   Strode, wallowed, ferreted, rampaged.

But acres crumple and the farm's new image
   Spreads over the old. As I face
   Its change, a truck tips litter; hens assess
Bright tins, then peck and squawk their rage.
   The truck spurts flame and I have no redress.

Todd

My father's white uncle became
   Arthritic and testamental in
   Lyrical stages. He held cardinal sin
Was misuse of horses, then any game

Won on the sabbath. A Clydesdale
   To him was not bells and sugar or declension
   From paddock, but primal extension
Of rock and soil. Thundered nail

Turned to sacred bolt. And each night
   In the stable he would slaver and slave
   At cracked hooves, or else save
Bowls of porridge for just the right

Beast. I remember I lied
   To him once, about oats: then I felt
   The brand of his loving tongue, the belt
Of his own horsey breath. But he died,

When the mechanised tractor came to pass.
   Now I think of him neighing to some saint
   In a simple heaven or, beyond complaint,
Leaning across a fence and munching grass.

Ferret

More vicious than stoat or weasel
Because caged, kept hungry, the ferrets
Were let out only for the kill:
An alternative to sulphur and nets.

Once one, badly mauled, hid
Behind a treacle-barrel in the shed.
Throwing me back, Matthew slid
The door shut. From outside

The window, I watched. He stood
Holding an axe, with no gloves.
Then it sprang; and his sleeves
Were drenched in blood

Where the teeth had sunk. I hear
Its high-pitched squeal,
The clamp of its neat steel
Jaws. And I still remember

How the axe flashed, severing
The ferret's head,
And how its body kept battering
The barrels, long after it was dead.

Farm Funeral

His hearse should have been drawn by horses.
That's what he envisaged: the strain
And clop of crupper and chain, flashing
Brass, fetlocks forcing high. With below
Him, the frayed sheets turning slowly yellow.

On the sideboard a silver cup he had won,
Inscribed 'to Todd Cochrane', now a lamp;
And tinted prints of his trotting days,
Switch in hand, jockey-capped, the gig silky
With light, wheels exquisitely spinning.

For fifty years he was a breeder of horses;
Nursing them nightly, mulling soft praise
Long after the vet would have driven his plunger in.
Yet through them was his hip split. Twice
He was crushed by a stallion rearing.

Himself to the end unbroken. God's tool, yes,
That to earth will return. But not before time.
He ought to have been conveyed to the grave
By clattering Clydesdales, not cut off
From lark and sorrel by unseemly glass.

The shire is sprinkled with his ashes.
The fields are green through his kind. Their clay,
His marrow. As much as the roisterer, he: even
That last ride to Craigie, boots tightly laced,
His tie held in place by a diamond pin.

Tremors

We took turns at laying
An ear on the rail —
So that we could tell
By the vibrations

When a train was coming.
Then we'd flatten ourselves
To the banks, scorched
Vetch and hedge-parsley,

While the iron flanks
Rushed past, sending sparks
Flying. It is more and more
A question of living

With an ear to the ground:
The tremors, when they come,
Are that much greater —
For ourselves, and others.

Nor is it any longer
A game, but a matter
Of survival: each explosion
Part of a procession

There can be no stopping.
Though the end is known,
There is nothing for it
But to keep listening . . .

Family Visit

Laying linoleum, my father spends hours
With his tape measure,
Littering the floor
As he checks his figures, gets
The angle right; then cuts
Carefully, to the music
Of a slow logic. In despair
I conjure up a room where
A boy sits and plays with coloured bricks.

My mind tugging at its traces,
I see him in more dapper days
Outside the Kibble Palace
With my grandfather, having
His snapshot taken; men firing
That year's leaves.
The Gardens are only a stone's throw
From where I live . . . But now
A younger self comes clutching at my sleeve.

Or off to Innellan, singing, we would go,
Boarding the steamer at the Broomielaw
In broad summer, these boomps-a-daisy
Days, the ship's band playing in a lazy
Swell, my father steering well clear
Of the bar, mother making neat
Packets of waste-paper to carry
To the nearest basket or (more likely)
All the way back to Cranworth Street.

Leaving my father at it
(He'd rather be alone) I take
My mother through the changed Botanics.
The bandstand is gone, and the great
Rain-barrels that used to rot
And overflow. Everything is neat
And plastic. And it is I who must walk
Slowly for her, past the sludge
And pocked marble of Queen Margaret Bridge.

'Kitchen-Maid'

Reaching the Rijksmuseum
mid-morning, in rain,
we skirt the main hall
with its tanned
tourists and guides

and, ignoring the rooms
we saw yesterday,
find ourselves heading
past Avercamp's skaters,
Breughel's masses of flowers,

and even the Night-Watch
in its noisy arena
till, up carpeted stairs,
we are in a chamber
made cool by Vermeer.

For what might be hours
we stand facing
a girl in a blue apron
pouring milk
from a brown jug.

Time comes to a stop.
Her gesture will stay
perpetually in place.
The jug will never empty,
the bowl never fill.

It is like seeing
a princess
asleep, under ice.
Your hand, brushing mine,
sustains the spell:

as I turn to kiss you,
we are ourselves
suspended in space;
your appraising glance
a passionate embrace.

Aquarium

Fishes striped like spinnakers
Bob towards us, then blousily
Go about. Theirs is a dark
World, haunted by bubbles.
Tapping the glass does nothing

To distract them, their steady
Intake. Press your face to it,
They merely distort further.
It is as though we were peering
Through a two-way mirror;

Underwater voyeurs, taking
The tide's pulse as well
As our own. Is this
How it will begin —
When the glaciers melt

And the caves refill?
How it will all end,
As we wait for the kill?
A face is imprinted
On the glass. An attendant,

Seeming scarcely to breathe,
Switches out the lights.
Luminous fronds unfurl.
Still no sound. Your ringed
Hand comes against mine, clutching.

Night Incident

Three nights running
you have wakened crying:

this time, because you heard
footsteps in your bedroom cupboard.

How do I help you understand
beyond

saying they are
from next door?

You calm down,
ask to see the moon.

It is full, tonight.
As we look out

I think of a lifetime
of haunted rooms,

of the violence
that is your inheritance.

I carry
you carefully

upstairs, and put
you in your cot;

then tiptoe to the door.
Your breathing is there, and no more.

Offshore

Edging from shingle, the dinghy turns
    A tight half-circle, heading past the island
With its twisted pines, the twin horns
    Of rock guarding the bay, out across the sound.

Opposite the lighthouse we ship the oars
    And drift, lopsided. The boys let out handlines,
Each hook hidden in plastic and red feathers:
    Preferable, they feel, to bait moiling in tins.

Each, thinking he has a bite, finds weed.
    Small hands grow icier, with each haul;
Until only hope deferred, and pride,
    Sustain them. I wish them mackerel —

But find my thoughts turn, coldly, towards
    The foreign fleets who come
Trawling our shores; recalling the words
    Of those who say this was a fishermen's kingdom

Once, the surface phosphorescent from shoals
    Of herring feeding; holds crammed,
Decks silver with their scales.
    A bygone age, not likely to return; the unnamed,

As is customary, having destroyed. The boys,
    Eyes glistening with weariness and trepidation,
Wind in for the last time. Grown wise,
    They know I know there's nothing on the line.

End of Season, Drumelzier

Scarcely discernible, the line tautens
Against the current, then sweeps downstream.
The rod-tip shifts, dislodging a thin
Gleam of light. I spool in, cast again.

So the season ends. In near darkness
I try to reach the rise.
Something jumps. The circles
Are absorbed. Night closes in.

I stumble from the luminescent Tweed,
And trudge by torchlight to the farm,
Then home: waders discarded, I concentrate
On the winding road; watch hedgerows pass,

Sheer banks; branches like weed, overhead.
Sedgeflies smudge the screen. I bear left
Towards row upon row of lights that never meet.
In under an hour, I am crossing Princes Street.

So the close of each trout season
Brings its own desperation
To make up for lost days; a trek
To the river, a casting more frantic

Than judged. In life and love too, take care
To make the most of time — before,
Darkness encroaching, it is too late
For anything but the final onslaught.

Douglas Dunn

Douglas Dunn, one of the leading poets of his generation, has lived for many years in England but is now back in Scotland. His poetry has an elegiac compassion, especially for those who are on the fringes of society: while his technical expertise is consummate. He has won many prizes for his poetry; and recently produced his first collection of short stories. His most recent book of poems *Elegies*, written after the death of his first wife, has been particularly well received.

Writing about my own writing is a task which I have had to perform several times before and I have always found it difficult. If I can say why, then I might elicit a note or two on the way in which I am concerned with poetry.

First, several strands of experience come together in poems, one or more of which is likely to be dominant, as well as personal or at the least subjective. Intimate feelings and events, whether relating to love, death, beliefs, or whatever, are the stuff of poetry, and poems are themselves intimate events generated by imagination and a kind of necessity. It is obedience to that necessity that makes a person a poet, or at any rate inclined towards writing poems. Once that event is over, and the poem written, then it often feels that to speak about that poem casually, or in a form extraneous to the poem itself, is somehow to demean it. All poets, I suppose, feel this to some extent; it so happens that I feel it increasingly.

I am not arguing for the privacy of poetry. One of my convictions is that a poem should not be so private as to be unapproachable by a reader. Obscurity in poetry is not a virtue, just as a lack of lucidity in prose is never to be thought commendable. But having said that, I must also admit that in poetry by others that I have come to admire, and in some poems of my own, experience and imagination together provoke imagery which adheres so naturally to the subject that its mysteriousness to the reader might be a response which I have to accept, in the hope that familiarity with the poem elucidates it in due course, in the same way that passages by other writers have been clarified for me by time and re-reading.

Although, then, I am conscious of writing for other people, and not for myself (except in the sense of attempting to live up to the notion of poetry given to me by reading and thinking), I believe in writing with the whole mind and the fullest exertion of whatever contemplative powers I possess. As well as feeling, which is probably the most important aspect of poetry, intelligence is also demanded of it. It is not as easy a formula in practice as it is to state. Brainy, cerebral poetry seldom recommends itself to me. The intelligence I'm referring to is a sentient, poetic one.

As for technique, I enjoy metre and rhyme. Although I do not despise 'free verse', my experience of it is that it encourages less freedom than its term suggests. Freedom to be melodic and lyric, to create cadences, to put a lilt to an image or picture, seem to me more important than the freedom to do without them. It is like freedom itself, real freedom: you make your own within the governing conventions, and hope that the institution — in this case, the institution of poetry, which is the tradition of poetry, the historic function of poetry — will protect you.

Douglas Dunn was born in 1942 and grew up at Inchinnan, in Renfrewshire. He went to the local primary school, Renfrew High School, and Camphill School, Paisley. He left school at seventeen and worked as a library assistant, spending a year at the Scottish School of Librarianship. He worked for a year in the U.S.A. After taking a degree in English at the University of Hull, he worked for a time in the university library there, and since 1971 he has earned his living as a freelance writer, moving back to live in Scotland, in Tayport, in 1984. As well as poetry, he writes short stories, radio plays, and he has written a TV play and several films for BBC TV using poetry for the soundtrack. The most recent of these was *Anon's People*. He has been awarded the Gregory Award, Somerset Maugham Award, Geoffrey Faber Memorial Prize and the Hawthornden Prize. His *Elegies* won the coveted Whitbread Award in 1985.

The Patricians

In small backyards old men's long underwear
Drips from sagging clotheslines.
The other stuff they take in bundles to the Bendix.

There chatty women slot their coins and joke
About the grey unmentionables absent.
The old men weaken in the steam and scratch at their rough chins.

Suppressing coughs and stiffnesses, they pedal bikes
On low gear slowly, in their faces
The effort to be upright, a dignity

That fits inside the smell of aromatic pipes.
Walking their dogs, the padded beats of pocket watches
Muffled under ancient overcoats, silences their hearts.

They live watching each other die, passing each other
In their white scarves, too long known to talk,
Waiting for the inheritance of the oldest, a right to power.

The street patricians, they are ignored.
Their anger proves something, their disenchantments
Settle round me like a cold fog.

They are the individualists of our time.
They know no fashions, copy nothing but their minds.
Long ago, they gave up looking in mirrors.

Dying in their sleep, they lie undiscovered.
The howling of their dogs brings the sniffing police,
Their middle-aged children from the new estates.

The Worst of All Loves

Where do they go, the faces, the people seen
In glances and longed for, who smile back
Wondering where the next kiss is coming from?

They are seen suddenly, from the top decks of buses,
On railway platforms at the tea machine,
When the sleep of travelling makes us look for them.

A whiff of perfume, an eye, a hat, a shoe,
Bring back vague memories of names,
Thingummy, that bloke, what's-her-name.

What great thing have I lost, that faces in a crowd
Should make me look at them for one I know,
What are faces that they must be looked for?

But there's one face, seen only once,
A fragment of a crowd. I know enough of her.
That face makes me dissatisfied with myself.

Those we secretly love, who never know of us,
What happens to them? Only this is known.
They will never meet us suddenly in pleasant rooms.

The Love Day

April, and young women glorify their flesh.
Their blushes warm their lovers' eyes.

The frisky toughs discard their heavy jackets,
Put on dark, sparse muscle-shirts.

Youth walks in couples nervous to cool bedrooms.
Some learn that love is not bad or permanent.

The ruffians are soft with their girlfriends.
They smile, keep their voices down, park their motorbikes.

Spring, the fugitives come to a stop here,
The thrush muffles its voice under the blossom,

Young husbands notice the flower shops,
The old men kiss their wives and long for their children.

It only lasts a day. After it, the insects come out.
Tender hands and mouths go back to eating.

Love Poem

I live in you, you live in me;
We are two gardens haunted by each other.
Sometimes I cannot find you there,
There is only the swing creaking, that you have just left,
Or your favourite book beside the sundial.

Landscape with One Figure

Shipyard cranes have come down again
To drink at the river, turning their long necks
And saying to their reflections on the Clyde,
"How noble we are."

The fields are waiting for them to come over.
Trees gesticulate into the rain;
Nerves of grasses quiver at their tips.
Come over and join us in the wet grass!

The wings of gulls in the distance wave
Like handkerchiefs after departing emigrants.
A tug sniffs up the river, looking like itself.
Waves fall from their small heights on river mud.

If I could sleep standing, I would wait here
Forever, become a landmark, something fixed
For tug crews or seabound passengers to point at,
An example of being a part of a place.

The Hunched

They will not leave me, the lives of other people.
I wear them near my eyes like spectacles.
The sullen magnates, hunched into chins and overcoats
In the back seats of their large cars;

The scholars, so conscientious, as if to escape
Things too real, names too easily read,
Preferring language stuffed with difficulties;
And children, furtive with their own parts;
A lonely glutton in the sunlit corner
Of an empty Chinese restaurant;
A coughing woman, leaning on a wall,
Her wedding ring finger in her son's cold hand,
In her back the invisible arch of death.
What makes them laugh, who lives with them?

I stooped to lace a shoe, and they all came back,
Dull, mysterious people without names or faces,
Whose lives I guess about, whose dangers tease.
And not one of them has anything at all to do with me.

After the War

The soldiers came, brewed tea in Snoddy's field
Beside the wood from where we watched them pee
In Snoddy's stagnant pond, small boys hidden
In pines and firs. The soldiers stood or sat
Ten minutes in the field, some officers apart
With the select problems of a map. Before,
Soldiers were imagined, we were them, gunfire
In our mouths, most cunning local skirmishers.
Their sudden arrival silenced. I lay down
On the grass and saw the blue shards of an egg
We'd broken, its warm yolk on the green grass,
And pine cones like little hand grenades.

One burst from an imaginary Browning,
A grenade well thrown by a child's arm,
And all these faces like our fathers' faces
Would fall back bleeding, trucks would burst in flames,
A blood-stained map would float on Snoddy's pond.
Our ambush made the soldiers laugh, and some
Made booming noises from behind real rifles
As we ran among them begging for badges,
Our plimsolls on the fallen May-blossom
Like boots on the faces of dead children.

But one of us had left. I saw him go
Out through the gate, I heard him on the road
Running to his mother's house. They lived alone,
Behind a hedge round an untended garden
Filled with broken toys, abrasive loss;
A swing that creaked, a rusted bicycle.
He went inside just as the convoy passed.

Guerrillas

They lived on farms, were stout and freckled, knew
Our country differently, from work, not play.
Fathers or brothers brought them to school in cars,
Dung on the doors, fresh eggs in the back.
The teachers favoured them for their wealth,
Daffodils and free eggs, and we envied them
The ownership of all the land we roved on,
Their dangerous dogs and stately horses,
The fruit we had to steal, their land being
Income, and ours a mysterious provider.
They owned the shadows cast by every branch,
Chestnuts and flowers, water, the awkward wire.
Their sullen eyes demanded rent, and so
We shouted the bad words to their sisters,
Threw stones at hens, blocked up the foggy drains.
Outlaws from dark woods and quarries,
We plundered all we envied and had not got,
As if the disinherited from farther back
Come to our blood like a knife to a hand.

Caledonian Moonlight

The white moon opens over a ridge of bracken
Spilling its prodigal rays into the eyes
Of the last pair of wildcat in the county
Looking for the kittens of their sterility
In the wiry heather

And the beautiful white face of a secretary
Rises in the shut eyes of a bachelor caretaker
Whose mother is dreaming
Of handing a plate of sandwiches to the minister

There are more moons in the night
Than eyes of those who see them
Open, venereal

Glasgow Schoolboys, Running Backwa:

High wind . . . They turn their backs to it, and push.
Their crazy strides are chopped in little steps.
And all their lives, like that, they'll have to rush
Forwards in reverse, always holding their caps.

Witch-girl

For evermore, they said, that girl was lame
In hands and feet, and that, they said, was proof
The lightless Devil spelled her into horse,
Moulding her hands and feet in solid hoof.

Poor girl, her mother saddled her, then rode
Through Sutherland until the outraged Law
Attended to the giddy-ups of gossip,
Force-feeding both of them on Tolbooth straw.

Only her mother was condemned. A pious mob —
Citizens and presbyters — whinnied, neighed,
Clip-clopped, as, standing in their fear of God,
There too were men who watched but also pitied.

Cold day in Dornoch . . . Shivering, the witch
Relieved her freezing round that fire which burned
To burn her up. Crowds psalmed with horror.
She blistered in the tar and, screaming, burned.

They spoke in Dornoch how the horses mourned
And how that lame girl, wandering, was heard
Tearing at the grass; and how she sat and sang,
As if the Devil also made her bird;

And how she washed her lameness in the rivers
From Oykell to the Clyde and Tweed and Forth,
Notorious as something to be pitied,
A girl to look at but a beast in worth.

No one could see her but would think he saw
Hoof in her fumbling hands, her staggering gait.
They spurned her flowers, as if they'd grown from her;
They barbed their righteous charity with hate.

She hawked her flowers in Glasgow, by the Trongate;
In Edinburgh, selling flowers, she slept
Beside the braziers of the City Guard.
The earth and animals within her wept.

No one to help her; no one saw her die,
If she is dead. By Gryfe, by Deveron,
By Cree and Tay, I see her wash her lameness,
And hear her breathing in the wood and stone.

Savings

She saved her money
And she hid her money in
An oriental tin
That came from Twining's Tea.
— 'Oh, how much money have you now?'
But she'd never let me see.
She'd place that tin into my hands,
Then with her hands on mine
She'd help me shake her Twining's tin —
Half-crowns and a sovereign,
Shillings, sixpences and florins
Rattled on the paper notes.

That was her funeral fund
I was too young to understand.
When I did, and she was dead,
It wasn't death that I could see
In tea-leaves sifting from a spoon
That came out of a Chinese tin.
I saw the life she'd shovelled in.

Leaving Dundee

A small blue window opens in the sky
As thunder rumbles somewhere over Fife.
Eight months of up-and-down — goodbye, goodbye —
Since I sat listening to the wild geese cry
Fanatic flightpaths up autumnal Tay,
Instinctive, mad for home — make way! make way!
Communal feathered scissors, cutting through
The grievous artifice that was my life,
I was alert again, and listening to
That wavering, invisible V-dart
Between two bridges. Now, in a moistened puff,
Flags hang on the château-stacked gables of
A 1980s expense account hotel,
A lost French fantasy, baronial.
From here, through trees, its Frenchness hurts my heart.
It slips into a library of times.
Like an eye on a watch, it looks at me.
And I am going home on Saturday
To my house, to sit at my desk of rhymes
Among familiar things of love, that love me.
Down there, over the green and the railway yards,
Across the broad, rain-misted, subtle Tay,
The road home trickles to a house, a door.
She spoke of what I might do "afterwards".
"Go, somewhere else." I went north to Dundee.
Tomorrow I won't live here any more,
Nor leave alone. *My love, say you'll come with me.*

Tom Leonard

Tom Leonard, born and brought up in Pollok in Glasgow, is one of the most refreshingly original poets in Scotland today. Proud of his working class roots, Tom Leonard is both scholarly and intellectual; his Dr Jekyll has however his Mr Hyde and the pull between himself and his *alter ego* gives that tension which provides the humour, the whimsy and the surprise, ever present in his work.

A radical, distrustful of sham, insincerity and political and religious hypocrisy, Tom Leonard satirises the Establishment, Big Business and mealy-mouthed Religion. Tom Leonard is acutely aware of the potency of language. For his football poems and Glasgow conversation pieces he presents his demotic language in an original phonetical manner. He is actively involved in the international Sound Poetry movement and this indeed influences his work.

I left school in 1962 aged seventeen. I had secretly been reading modern poetry at home for about two years, since I'd first come across Stephen Spender's poem 'The Express', which had completely 'sent' me, as the word then was.

I say I had 'secretly' been reading modern poetry, as it was in those days not at all uncommon for schools to ignore all living poets as producers of worthless formless bunkum. This suited me fine, as it led me to read contemporary British and American poetry with that particular keenness with which one consumes forbidden fruit. Had I been born twenty years later, I doubt if I would have left my school without having written at least one essay beginning, 'My favourite living Scottish poet is . . .' Whether I would subsequently have gone on myself to write poems, I don't know.

The American poets who interested me most were e. e. cummings and William Carlos Williams. People whose work I've subsequently been particularly keen on, at different times, have been Beckett, Robbe-Grillett, Ian Hamilton Finlay, Bob Cobbing, Dunbar, 'BV' Thomson, Brecht. I've also had a thing about Mayakovsky's formal daring since reading him in translation in my teens: words I think of in connection with these writers are 'verve' and 'commitment'. Most of them too would not be thought of as part of the 'mainstream' of poetry by contemporary British literary critics. Most would also be considered 'extremist'.

In terms of actual technical influences on my work — as distinct from my areas of personal literary taste — I suspect that music has had at least as much influence as anything else. That's why I called my selected poems *Intimate Voices 1965–83*: the title refers not simply to the fact that the poems in the book use different voices and registers, but also to the name of a string quartet by Sibelius. Another influence I'd say is that which I do recall from my schooldays with most pleasure — geometry. I remember finding the proofs to the propositions very satisfying; I also remember feeling particular satisfaction if I could find a way of proving a proposition by different methods from that shown by the teacher, or the book.

Born Glasgow 1944. Variety of clerical jobs, spells of unemployment, lengthy spell at Glasgow University where he did postgraduate work on James Thomson ('BV'). Presently (1985) Writer in Residence to Renfrew District Libraries.

The Good Thief

> heh jimmy
> yawright ih
> stull wayiz urryi
> ih
>
> heh jimmy
> ma right insane yirra pape
> ma right insane yirwanny uz jimmy
> see it nyir eyes
> wanny uz

heh

heh jimmy
lookslik wirgonny miss thi gemm
gonny miss thi GEMM jimmy
nearly three a cloke thinoo

dork init
good jobe they've gote thi lights

Paroakial

thahts no whurrits aht
thahts no cool man
jiss paroakial

aw theez sporran heads
tahty scoan vibes
thi haggis trip

bad buzz man
dead seen

goahty learna new langwij
sumhm ihnturnashnl
Noah Glasgow hangup
bunnit husslin

gitinty elektroniks man
really blow yir mine
real good blast
no whuhta mean

mawn
turn yirself awn

A Summer's Day

yir eyes ur
eh
a mean yir

pirrit this wey
ah a thingk yir
byewtifl like ehm

fact
fact a thingk yir
ach a luvyi thahts

thahts
jist thi wey it iz like
thahts ehm
aw ther iz ti say

The Voyeur

what's your favourite word dearie
is it wee
I hope it's wee
wee's such a nice wee word
like a wee hairy dog
with two wee eyes
such a nice wee word to play with dearie
you can say it quickly
with a wee smile
and a wee glance to the side
or you can say it slowly dearie
with your mouth a wee bit open
and a wee sigh dearie
a wee sigh
put your wee head on my shoulder dearie
oh my
a great wee word
and Scottish
it makes you proud

Fireworks

up cumzthi wee man
beats three men
slingzowra crackir

an Lennux
aw yi wahntia seenim
coolizza queue cumbir

bump

rightnthi riggin
poastij stamp
a rockit

that wuzzit
that wuzthi end

finisht

Feed Ma Lamz

Amyir gaffirz Gaffir. Hark.

nay fornirz ur communists
nay langwij
nay lip
nay laffn ina sunday
nay g.b.h. (septina wawr)
nay nooky huntn
nay tea-leaven
nay chanty rasslin
nay nooky huntn nix doar
nur kuvitn their ox

Oaky doaky. Stick way it
— rahl burn thi lohta yiz.

Prisoner in thi Bar

would thi prisoner
in thi bar
please stand

fur thi aforesaid crime
uv writn anuthir poem
awarded thi certificate of safety
by thi scottish education department

fit tay be used in schools
huvn no bad language
sex subversion or antireligion

I hereby sentence you
tay six munths hard labour
doon nthi poetry section
uv yir local library
coontn thi fuckin metaphors

Four of the Belt

Jenkins, all too clearly it is time
for some ritual physical humiliation;
and if you cry, boy, you will prove
what I suspect — you are not a man.

As they say, Jenkins, this hurts me
more than it hurts you. But I show you
I am a man, by doing this, to you.

When *you* are a man, Jenkins, you may hear
that physical humiliation and ritual
are concerned with strange adult matters
— like rape, or masochistic fantasies.

You will not accept such stories.
Rather, you will recall with pride,
perhaps even affection, that day when I,
Mr. Johnstone, summoned you before me,
and gave you four of the belt

like this. And this. And this. And this.

From: A Priest came on at Merkland Street

A
very thoughtful poem,
being a canonical penance
for sufferers of psychosomatic asthma.

oh no
holy buttons
sad but dignified
and sitting straight across from me
a troubled soul
my son
christ
a bit of Mahler's Seventh might drown him
dah dum, da dum dah dee,
dah dah dah DAH da dah
da DAH, dah DEE da da da
DUM DUM dah dee
hello there
when I'm dead
when I think I'm dead
and I'm in my box
and it's all dark
and I'm wondering where the air's coming from
I'll see this curtain
and it will move to the side
and your great horrible leering face
how many times my son
and how long ago was this
bless me father for I am tinned
christ

maybe he's saying hail mary's
maybe he's praying for all the souls in purgatory
and really sincere
the nicest man in the world
he really loves people
hello father
I'm going to give you a smile
I'm going to give you the nicest smile in the world
it will be real love
there will be absolutely no sex
we will both be five years old
and we'll go to school together
play at weekends together
and you'll climb inside my box
laughing

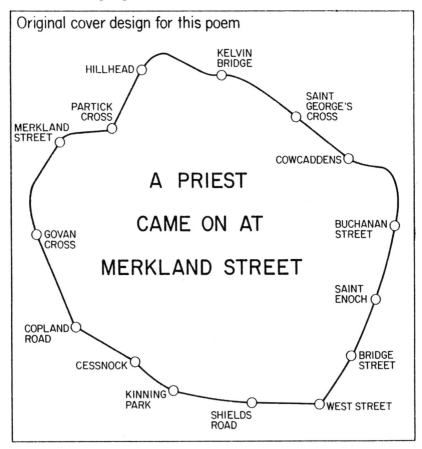

Original cover design for this poem

KELVIN BRIDGE

HILLHEAD

PARTICK CROSS

SAINT GEORGE'S CROSS

MERKLAND STREET

COWCADDENS

A PRIEST

CAME ON AT

MERKLAND STREET

GOVAN CROSS

BUCHANAN STREET

SAINT ENOCH

COPLAND ROAD

CESSNOCK

BRIDGE STREET

KINNING PARK

WEST STREET

SHIELDS ROAD

lying together in the dark
innocent as hell
like after lights out in a school dormitory
cosy but exciting
and maybe God will look round the curtain
hello there
softly as God would say it
and we'll all go away together
away through his door
for ever
amen
I always spoil it
but maybe you'd spoil it yourself
maybe you wouldn't be five years old at all
and you'd climb inside my box
a troubled soul
my son
with a keyhole in your back
wind me up in the morning
and a button under your right arm
how many times my son
and a button under your left arm
how long ago was this
and a button in the back of your head
press to bless
and a tape recorder between your ears
from henceforth ye shall catch men
from henceforth ye shall catch men
from henceforth ye shall catch men
dah dum, da dum dah dee,
oh no
you won't catch me
maybe I'll be really dead
as dead as everyone else who has died
just lying in a box
a box that somebody's made
a box for dead people
and I won't even know
christ

my name is Ozymandias
king of Leithland Road
Pollok
Glasgow SW3
and all the worrying
all the wanting to be five years old
imagine
the lone and level
far away
amen
only it's not the lone and level at all
for there's the Lansdowne Clinic for Functional Nervous Disorders
and the Southern General Hospital Department of Psychological Medicine
and Leverndale formerly known as Hawkhead Mental Asylum
I could write to a psychiatrist
a cry from the heart
dear sir
my name is Ozymandias
king of Leithland Road
and then there's the box
yours sincerely
maybe faithfully would be better
you know who
ps
I always spoil it
pps
I am awful lonely
ppps
I don't know what people are for
oh no
maybe I think about the box too much
maybe nobody else thinks about the box at all
at least not for long
not more than five minutes a day
or maybe ten minutes at the weekend
and that's all they need

The Qualification

wurk aw yir life
nuthnty show
pit oanthi nyuze
same awl drivl

yoonyin bashn
wurkir bashn
lord this
sir soan soa thaht

shood hearma boay
sayzwi need gunz
an armd revalooshn
nuthn else wurks

awright fur him thoa
uppit thi yooni*
tok aw yi like therr
thats whit its fur

university

The Dropout

scrimpt nscraipt furryi
urryi grateful
no wan bit

speylt useless yi urr
twistid izza coarkscrew
cawz rowz inan empty hooss

yir fathir nivirid yoor chance
pick n choozyir joab
a steady pey

well jiss take a lookit yirsell
naithur wurk nur wahnt
aw aye

yir clivir
damm clivir
but yi huvny a clue whutyir dayn

Non Sum Qualis Eram Bonae Sub Regn Cynarae

between the kisses
and the wine

and the wee heavies
and the newcastle browns
and the special brews
and the half bottles of grouse
and the merrydown cider
and the bell's
and the whyte & mackay's
and the dewar's
and the glen grant's
and the glen moranje's
and the odd bottle of old england
and the nembies
and the acid
and the moroccan grass

I have been faithful to thee, Cynara!
in my fashion

From: Unrelated Incidents

(3)

this is thi
six a clock
news thi
man said n
thi reason
a talk wia
BBC accent
iz coz yi
widny wahnt
mi ti talk
aboot thi
trooth wia
voice lik
wanna yoo
scruff. if
a toktaboot
thi trooth
lik wanna yoo
scruff yi
widny thingk
it wuz troo.
jist wanna yoo
scruff tokn.
thirza right
way ti spell
ana right way
ti tok it. this
is me tokn yir
right way a
spellin. this
is ma trooth.
yooz doant no
thi trooth
yirsellz cawz
yi canny talk
right. this is
the six a clock
nyooz. belt up.

(6)

its aw thi
fault a
thi unions hi
said n thi
wurkirs beein
too greedy
hi added n
thi commies n
no inuff
moderates stonnin
upn gettin
coontid n
lame ducks gitn
whut huvyi
bailt oot n
white elifints
getn selt doon
thi river n
a mean
wiv goat tay
puhll in
wur belts n
wur bax ur
tay thi waw
yiv goat tay
admit it.

then hi took
ootiz nummer
eight n
geen a luvvly
wee chip up
right
biside thi flag
n tapptit doon
furra three:

a burdie.

don't tell wordsworth

she dwelt among the untrodden ways
and went her messages by helicopter

Placenta

Good-bye to that good woman
who fed you life through a cord
and pushed you into the world:

leave go the rope —
let the weight of her body
leave you. Let the grave

be stitched up. In nine months
the scar will be invisible.

Liz Lochhead

Liz Lochhead, whose origins are in the central belt of Scotland, is clearly one of the most talented Scottish poets today. At school, she already enjoyed writing although she turned to her other love, painting, for a career, graduating from the Glasgow School of Art. One of her poems, 'On the inadequacy of a sketch at Millport Cathedral', suggests that she finds words her ideal means of communication. She is a keen observer of her fellow women and men but is not averse to taking herself down at times. At the same time she is an expert story teller. She is firmly, though not assertively, feminist. Widely travelled in Canada and the United States, she has been frequently engaged as Writer in Residence, giving valuable advice and encouragement to the young in creative writing.

When I look back over the things I've written I can see shifts in my themes, obsessions and sources that, of course, I wasn't necessarily aware of at the time.

The early things in *Memo for Spring* attempted to make over again the places and especially the people — family, neighbours — of the Lanarkshire home which I was at nineteen, twenty, twenty-one, breaking away from; and celebrated my to-me new and exciting relationship with Glasgow in the late sixties, early seventies. My internal manifesto was for the ordinary and the here-and-now. Although not at all consciously aware of it, I was making a young and a particularly female persona, I think.

As I read more and lived more I became much more conscious of femaleness and how — in Graves' metaphor of the White Goddess for instance — the 'female' was always the 'other' the hunted-for 'object' of most poetry. Of all true poetry, he says. I became interested in how the female poet — especially if she wasn't Sappho — could forge any sort of Muse for herself. For me this meant a going inward, trusting the pull of familiar mother-tongue legendary, folk-tale oral traditions and making exactly the sort of 'allusive' poetry I had scorned and sworn to avoid in *Memo for Spring*. A lot of them came out as wisecracking out-loud poems, masks like the masks they tried to be about, as I attempted to take on stereotypes as well as archetypes, slap-happily collaging women's magazine clichés and Grimm's *Household Tales* — all good 'folk' material, it seemed to me, all part of the luggage I carried around. This did not always work. Women found them truer and therefore funnier than men did.

I feel they were certainly assertively and un-apologetically 'feminist' and the longer I live in Scotland the more assertively feminist — in the sense of longing for 'womanly values' in both men and women in this repressed, violent, colonised society — I get.

Currently I am writing in different ways about ambivalence, repression, the 'thrill' of terror and the 'responsibility' of the maker. A black, black-humoured demonic Male Muse begins to emerge . . . I don't know what poems I'll write next.

Liz Lochhead was born in Motherwell in 1947. She trained as a painter in Glasgow College of Art and then worked in schools as a Teacher of Art for eight years. A year of exchange to Canada on a Scottish/Canadian writers fellowship in 1978 induced her to become a full-time writer. She travels widely in Britain giving readings. She has written two successful plays on the macabre themes of Dracula and Frankenstein and has collaborated in a number of revues in Glasgow and elsewhere.

What the Pool Said, on Midsummer's Day

I've led you by my garrulous banks, babbling
on and on till — drunk on air
and sure it's only water talking —
you come at last to my silence.
Listen, I'm dark
and still and deep enough.
Even this hottest gonging sun
on this longest day
can't white me out.

What are you waiting for?
I lie here, inviting, winking you in.

The woman was easy.
Like to like, I called her, she came.
In no time I had her
out of herself, slipping on my water-stockings,
leaning into, being cupped and clasped
in my green glass bra.
But it's you I want, and you know it, man.
I watch you, stripped, knee-deep
in my shallows, telling yourself
that what makes you gasp
and balls your gut
is not my coldness but your own fear.

— Your reasonable fear,
what's true in me admits it.
(Though deeper, oh
older than any reason).
Yes, I could
drown you, you
could foul my depths, it's not
unheard of. What's fish
in me could make flesh of you,
my wet weeds against your thigh, it
could turn nasty.
I could have you
gulping fistfuls fighting yourself
back from me.

I get darker and darker, suck harder.
On-the-brink man, you
wish I'd flash and dazzle again.
You'd make a fetish of zazzing dragonflies?
You want I should zip myself up
with the kingfisher's flightpath, be beautiful?
I say no tricks. I say just trust,
I'll soak through your skin and
slake your thirst.

I watch. You clench,
clench and come into me.

In the Dreamschool

you are never the teacher.
The history lesson
goes on for ever.

Yammering the always
wrong answer to the hardest question
You stand up in nothing but
a washed-in vest.

In the dreamschool nothing can be covered up.
Fleeced, yellowing
you never learn.

Teacher is bigeyed behind
awesome bifocals
and his teeth are green.
An offered apple will only tempt the snake
curled under his chalkstripe jacket. Loch-
gelly, forked tongue, tawse.

Moonfaced mongols drag you towards
The terrible lavatories.

Sawdust soaks up sour mistakes.

The Offering

Never in a month of them
would you go back.
Sunday,
the late smell of bacon
then the hard small feeling
of the offering in the mitten.
Remember how the hat-elastic cut.
Oh the boredom,
and how a lick of spittle got purple dye or pink
from the hymn-book you worried.

Maybe your neighbour would
have technicoloured pictures of
Jesus curing lepers
between the frail tissue pages of her bible
or she'd stroke you with the velvet
of a pressed rosepetal
till someone sucking peppermint
and smelling of mothball
poked you and hissed that you weren't to fidget.
Remember the singing
(with words and actions)
and how you never quite
understood the one about Nic-
odemus Coming to the Lord by Night.

Sunday,
perhaps an auntie
would visit with a cousin. Every Sunday
everyone would eat ice cream
and your mothers would compare you,
they'd stand you by the doorstop
and measure you up.

Sunday, maybe later in the evening
There'd be a Brethren Meeting.
Plain women wearing hats to cover
uncut hair. And
singing, under lamp-posts, out in our street.
And the leader
shouted the odds on Armageddon, he
tried to sell Salvation.
Everybody turned their televisions up.

Never in a month of them
should you go back.
Fond hope.
you'll still find you do not measure up.
The evangelist still mouths behind glass unheard.
You'll still not understand
the singing, the action or the word.
Ice cream will cloy, too sweet, to bland.
And the offering
still hard and knotted in your hand.

Spinster

This is no way to go on.
Get wise. Accept. Be
a spinster of this parish.
My life's in shards.
I will keep fit in leotards.

Go vegetarian. Accept.
Support good causes.
Be frugal, circumspect.
Keep cats. Take tidy fits.
Go to evening classes.
Keep a nest-egg in the bank.
Try Yoga. Cut your losses.
Accept. Admit you're a bit of a crank —

Oh I may be a bit of a crank
but still I get by, frugally. Think positive.
I live and let live. Depend
on nobody. Accept.
Go in for self-improvement.
Keep up with trends.
I'll cultivate my conversation.
I'll cultivate my friends.
I'll grow a herbaceous border.
By hook by crook I'll get my house in order.

From: Three Twists

I. Rapunzstiltskin

& just when our maiden had got
good & used to her isolation,
stopped daily expecting to be rescued,
had come to almost love her tower,
along comes This Prince
with absolutely
all the wrong answers.

Of course she had not been brought up to look for
originality or gingerbread
so at first she was quite undaunted
by his tendency to talk in strung-together cliché.
'Just hang on and we'll get you out of there'
he hollered like a fireman in some soap opera
when she confided her plight (the old
hag inside etc. & how trapped she was);
well, it was corny but
he did look sort of gorgeous
axe and all.
So there she was, humming & pulling
all the pins out of her chignon,
throwing him all the usual lifelines
till, soon, he was shimmying in & out
every other day as though
he owned the place, bringing her
the sex manuals & skeins of silk
from which she was meant, eventually,
to weave the means of her own escape.
'All very well & good,' she prompted,
'but when exactly?'
She gave him till
well past the bell on the timeclock.
She mouthed at him, hinted,
she was keener than a T.V. quizmaster
that he should get it right.
'I'll do everything in my power' he intoned, 'but
the impossible (she groaned) might
take a little longer.' He grinned.
She pulled her glasses off.
'All the better
to see you with my dear?' he hazarded.
She screamed, cut off her hair.
'Why, you're beautiful?' he guessed tentatively.
'No, No, No!' she
shrieked & stamped her foot so
hard it sank six cubits through the floorboards.
'I love you?' he came up with
as finally she tore herself in two.

My Mother's Suitors

have come to court me
have come to call oh
yes with their wonderful world
war two moustaches their long
stem roses their cultivated
accents (they're English aren't they
at very least they're
educated-Scots).
They are absolutely
au fait with menu-French
they know the language of flowers
& oh they'd die
rather than send a dozen yellow
they always get them right & red.
Their handwriting on the florist's card
slants neither too much to the left or right.

They are good sorts.
They have the profile for it — note
the not too much nose
the plenty chin. The
stockings they bring have no strings
& their square
capable hands are forever
lifting your hair and gently
pushing your head away from them
to fumble endearingly at your nape
with the clasp of the pretty heirloom
little necklace they know their
grandmother would have wanted
you to have.
(never opals — they know
that pearls mean tears).

They have come to call & we'll all
go walking under the black sky's
droning big bombers
among the ratatat of ack-ack.

We'll go dancing & tonight
shall I wear the lilac, or the
scarlet, or the white?

Laundrette

We sit nebulous in steam.
It calms the air and makes the windows stream
rippling the hinterland's big houses to a blur
of bedsits — not a patch on what they were before.

We stuff the tub, jam money in the slot,
sit back on rickle chairs not
reading. The paperbacks in our pockets curl.
Our eyes are riveted. Our own colours whirl.

We pour in smithereens of soap. The machine sobs
through its cycle. The rhythm throbs
and changes. Suds drool and slobber in the churn.
Our duds don't know which way to turn.

The dark shoves one man in,
lugging a bundle like a wandering Jew. Linen
washed in public here.
We let out of the bag who we are.

This youngwife has a fine stack of sheets, each pair
a present. She admires their clean cut air
of colourschemes and being chosen. Are the dyes fast?
This christening lather will be the first test.

This woman is deadpan before the rinse and sluice
of the family in a bagwash. Let them stew in their juice
to a final fankle, twisted, wrung out into rope,
hard to unravel. She sees a kaleidoscope

For her to narrow her eyes and blow smoke at, his overalls
and pants ballooning, tangling with her smalls
and the teeshirts skinned from her wriggling son.
She has a weather eye for what might shrink or run.

This dour man does for himself. Before him,
half lost, his small possessions swim.
Cast off, random
they nose and nudge the porthole glass like flotsam.

Revelation

I remember once being shown the black bull
when a child at the farm for eggs and milk.
They called him Bob — as though perhaps
you could reduce a monster
with the charm of a friendly name.
At the threshold of his outhouse, someone
held my hand and let me peer inside.
At first, only black
and the hot reek of him. Then he was immense,
his edges merging with the darkness, just
a big bulk and a roar to be really scared of,
a trampling, and a clanking tense with the chain's jerk.
His eyes swivelled in the great wedge of his tossed head.
He roared his rage. His nostrils gaped.

And in the yard outside,
oblivious hens picked their way about.
The faint and rather festive tinkling
behind the mellow stone and hasp was all they knew
of that Black Mass, straining at his chains.
I had always half-known he existed —
this antidote and Anti-Christ his anarchy
threatening the eggs, well rounded, self-contained —
and the placidity of milk.

I ran, my pigtails thumping on my back in fear,
past the big boys in the farm lane
who pulled the wings from butterflies and
blew up frogs with straws.
Past throned hedge and harried nest,
scared of the eggs shattering —
only my small and shaking hand on the jug's rim
in case the milk should spill.

After a Warrant Sale

I watched her go,
Ann-next-door
(dry eyed,
as dignified
as could be expected)
the day after they came,
sheriff court men
with the politeness of strangers
impersonally
to rip her home apart —
to tear her life along the dotted line
officially.

On the sideboard that went for fifteen bob,
a photograph.
Wedding-day Walter and
Ann: her hair was lightened,
and her, with hopes.
No-one really knows
when it began to show —
trouble, dark roots.

It was common knowledge
there were faults on both sides,
and the blame —
whether it was over drink
or debt no-one seems to know,
or what was owing to exactly whom.
Just in the end the warrant sale,
and Ann's leaving.

But what seemed strange:
I wondered why,
having stayed long past the death of love
and the ashes of hope,
why pack it up and go
over some sticks of furniture
and the loss of one's only partially
paid-for washing machine?

Those who are older tell me,
after a married year or two
the comforts start to matter
more than the comforting.
But I am very young,
expecting not too much of love —
just that it should completely solve me.
And I can't understand.

Valerie Gillies

Valerie Gillies has emerged in recent years as one of the most promising of the younger poets. Along with her exotic and colourful poems about India she has some lovely sensuous poems about children and childhood which have a feminine tenderness and exactitude.

My grandparents' house was on the Lanarkshire moors. The sound of spoken Scots meant escape from school in Edinburgh. The tawny uplands, the overgrown shale bings, the hill farms, the fields with the rain moving in: these scenes made me a writer. By the age of fourteen I began to celebrate animal energy in poems. I was fascinated by movement, putting it into the dynamics of poetry, whether in strict form or freer verse. The book *Bed of Stone* I named after the greatest greyhound ever.

While I read English at Edinburgh University, Norman MacCaig was Writing Fellow there, and he encouraged me to keep writing. I spent long hours talking to Sorley MacLean, who was then headmaster of a high school in Wester Ross, and these conversations inspired me to read our Scots poets, and to learn enough Gaelic to explore the wealth of Gaelic literature.

I was awarded a Commonwealth Scholarship to live in India to study contemporary writers such as Raja Rao and Narayan. In Mysore I was the only European at the university. India adopted me and I vanished up country.

Returning to Scotland I wrote a thesis on the poetry of William Drummond of Hawthornden. I married a Celtic scholar, and we have three children and a house where, in between the sounds of play and quarrel, music can be heard, the Scots fiddle and the clarsach.

Once I had all my time to myself, in the wilds of Mysore State, to think clearly. Now I am a harassed housewife without respite. There is a stressful world full of negative energies around us. But poetry continues: I re-read the living breath of the Scots ballads, I hear the voices of Pound, Yeats, Hardy, Edward Thomas, Seamus Heaney. I believe in Feinstein's translations of the great Russian women poets of this century, especially Tsvetayeva.

I go to tutor young writers in schools, and in seven years no two visits have been the same, until I have seen the richness that lies in each one of us who wants to write.

Valerie Gillies was born in Canada in 1948 but brought up in Scotland. Her higher education was at the universities of Edinburgh and Mysore, southern India. She has lived for nine years in Edinburgh writing radio scripts, revues, commissioned books and poetry. She has had published two books of poetry. She is married to the Professor of Celtic at Edinburgh University and combines the work of writer with running a household and bringing up two children.

Native

The first stir of a southern autumn
And how I missed Scotland;
A restlessness for those quiet purples begun
When my eyes wanted all light shunned

Save that shining from the skies' grace
Upon our own homeland, the heart's place;
I am to my country
A leaf on which the likeness of the tree is traced.

Asian in Edinburgh

Far off
in the crowd
a sleek oriental head —
assumption of calm
not borne out
when the traffic closes
with grave foglamps
in the puritan manner

And nearer
their wolfskin caps.

Through
an alien street odour,
its reticent fumes,
the stranger moves
all gold
his nape delicate
inclined towards the station steps;
each step a slight regret
below the quietest of suns.

El Greco Painting

It is to desire this perfection of white,
To change the rust of our jewel to green
That the man rose half-mad from the night
To translate Toledo from dust to light.

Ah, a light to dissolve the dark,
Leaping from the bodies of men
Whose eyes can weep, leaving no mark,
No stain on the neck, the thighs denying dark.

Could we all receive this affliction, blind
To the seeming colour of the sky, the sad!
But then of course the man was mad
Painting as a good pupil should
Until his brain could break that mood,
Dream a way out of the dark and be glad.

Identifying You

What on earth
compares with you?

Not the sun who
is close to the eastern
edge of things.
Your eyes regard him, unblinking.

Not the moon who
comes with dark and
does great damage.
You make shards of her vessel.

Not the wind who
roars like a blast
from the blessed land.
You keep this place warm against him.

Not the rain who
whispers our sins are
refusals to get wet.
Your hair gives colour to dry-stacked hay.

Not our children who
are frosthaloed stars
brightening us by delusions.
You have a wintry way with you.

What on earth
compares with you?

Hibernator

My child's flesh, after the bath,
smells sweet as the thaw
must, to hibernating creatures.

While I washed him
I was the winter-wind in action
of attrition: he emerged a landform.

Now, drying him with the bleached towel,
I am that she-bear who licks her cub,
moulding it to its true shape to come.

For a Son's First Birthday

You were a Moses striking rock.
I let out the life
that wanted to come.

What I forget
is that restiveness:
there was the true childbed.

I watched the back of your head come:
that much form
let me know you were a son.

No bald pate, but a full head of hair;
the appearance of your scalp unfolding
the reality of a new mind within.

Born wringing wet as the moorlands,
you were blue
as blaeberry behind their leaves.

Your first breath
blew you up so pink
you were ragged robin in the marshes.

What I forget
is your first sound:
loud, brilliant and reedy.

Rising Early

Rising early, I can remember
what it was like
when I had a child's eye level,
only so high above the ground.

In that dimension
I felt the walled garden
as no adult can do,
for I had to tilt my head
right back, to see
my grandmother's window.

The many other windows
in the building seemed
stunned by their smoke of emptiness,
but in hers, a dull yellow
shone around her.
Her hand so active
at the sink, paused, and waved.

Right up to today
I am the same girl
to my grandmother.
The love between us travels across
in a moving whole of silence
like any bird,
and as if surrounded
by the high window-way glow,
we are only a wave apart.

For Surah

I always had a dog,
but you were the one
who embodied my own spirit.
I would love to have been you;
simple, swift, beautiful
till the day you died.

I picture myself as you:
cherished and important
throughout five thousand years
since the first cave-painter at Balk
held back the deerhound tightly.

I want to see you again
as you were, looking straight at me.
Perhaps a red pollen of blood.
dusts your muzzle, in heaven;
perhaps some hare in eternity
scents a hound on the little breeze.

If it should run from you
as you are, the hare's heart will burst,
immortal or not; you are off the leash
now, who kept death on a tether
tied to you; where you went,
death and beauty ran together.

Bantam

He's a bantam cockerel
in a speckled jumper,
hotly disputing
each move the other boys make.

A little boy from the street
whose hair bristles like feathers
tied up in the war-bonnet
of a cockerel's crest and comb.

His gymshoe frays on a spurred foot
first in the flurry of kicks.
His punches wing to the heads
of friends and enemies alike.

No matter how big they seem
he is up and at them
as a brief fight bursts out:
bantams battering above long grass.

Damp, volatile after the swimming-pool,
his fingers point like spikes.
Pie-crust juts from his beak,
his eye a black cock's eye.

Bird energy flaps his clothes,
his ragged towel tailing him in the skirmish:
when he's run on,
it lies motionless as a feather.

The Black Bike

Wearer of a blue Afghan turban
above magnificent features,
he kept on the old warlike look.

He became my best friend.
He'd made up his mind about that
when we met, riding on the racecourse.

Changing from horse to motorbike
gives the balance a queer turn.
My knees had to stop gripping.

For a year we roamed the south
on the black Norton together,
my crash-helmet an oven.

We saw the mosque from the outside
and that field where a Parsee pulled
my father from the fiery wreck in '42.

Yes, I had a great view of India:
it was all your broad back, Manzoor,
and villagers waving to the black bike.

Heirloom for a Young Boy

This is what he wanted you to have:
a military cap
with peak and strap,
marked "1915" inside.

Long vacant,
it suddenly
so suddenly descends
like an iron band around a skull,
ringingly.
In the shadow of its peak
your eyes sink
to take their own tour of the battlefields.

You give out his level look
and now tip me his wink.
Come away, resemblance:
teeth face bones joints outline gait smile
astonish me!

His image I loved, I see in you,
and you (all him) have all the all of youth.

The Old Empress

Indira Gandhi in April 1977

As she says her farewell
she gives a smile.
She isn't missing a thing.

Is it good enough?

She is weathering the worst
accorded to any living lady.
Loathing falls on her like a hard rain.

Pilloried as a traitor,
hanged in effigy,
now convicted at a mock trial:

will she come out of it?

In the South they still love her,
but in Delhi it will soon be night;
puffy old roses are brimful of rain.

Roadgang Women

Here come the stonebreakers,
these little skeletons of the roadgang women
with their long strands of hair
knotted high at the back of their skulls.

They take a moment
to wipe sweat from around their eyes
with a corner of torn sari.
The road waits for their hands.

They carry stones in baskets on their heads,
like apricots marked by a bird's beak,
wizened and bruised:
both heads and stones.

A raised track on a country without limit.
A big sun beating off any shade.
A woman stitches a piece of shadow
with an upright stick and sacking.

She breaks stones below it.
Once, she eats from a shallow tin dish
with not much in it;
some steamed riceflour cake.

Old women of thirty
work in the day's quickforge.
Nobody can work like them,
though they pause to quarrel or laugh.

They must find fire nourishing,
as the salamander does, who is meant
to live in the flames, who feeds on her death:
where others would die, she lives happily.

Cigarette in the Bath

Nobody said
and nothing I've read
told me what it was going to be like.
He looked so small last night
and ugly, but what with the epidural I had
the birth was not too bad.
The worst is, now I've got scared,
they've taken him into intensive care.
They've showed me him, looking damp,
eyes bandaged, going under the lamp.
He's scrunched up tight with lifesavers
all wired up in the incubator.
I want to walk out, it's not fair,
I mean, he could stay there
and I could just go
off if I want to, on my own.
There are different things, they say,
wrong with him, anyway.
But when I see him try,
he really tries
to draw the bliss of breath.
So I stay, I can't forget it.

The Old Woman's Reel

She is at the small deep window
looking through and out:
the Aran islands, rock and seawater,
lie all about.
A face strong in poverty's hauteur
is hers, then and now.

Being a young woman in Flaherty's film
"Man of Aran",
she nearly drowned in the undertow
by the boat where she ran.
He kept on filming even though
he thought her dead on the rockrim.

A body plaited by water twine
they carried ashore:
partnered in the ocean's set dance
by two men or more.
The sea had had its chance
to peel her off by the shoreline.

Now in her great old age
toothless and tough,
the island music still delights her:
one dance is not enough.
The tunes of a people poor and cut off there
have a special power to engage.

Drawn upright, her stiff bones
already dancing,
she spins, not on one foot
but on her stick, tap-balancing.
While to one side like a pliant offshoot
a little girl mimics her, unbeknown.

Notes

G. S. Fraser

15 *Meditation of a Patriot*
Compton Mackenzie (1883–1972) famous Scottish novelist.
'St Andrews soothes that critic': this almost certainly refers to Edwin Muir (1887–1959).

16 *To Hugh MacDiarmid*
Mithridates VI (120–63 BC) King of Pontus, Asia Minor, a valiant opponent of the Roman Empire.

18 *Home Town Elegy*
Carden Place: Aberdeen street near Aberdeen Grammar School at which Byron and G. S. Fraser were both educated.

19 *Christmas Letter Home*
Rostov (on Don): scene of fierce fighting when Hitler invaded Russia in World War II.

George Campbell Hay

35 *Bizerta*: scene of battle in Tunisia in World War II.

W. S. Graham

55 *The Nightfishing*
A part of this poem is represented here. On one level purely descriptive of a night at sea, at another level it is a meditation on poetry and language, indeed on problems of communication of the poet's experience.

59 *I leave this at your ear*
A love poem to the poet's wife.

Derick Thomson

69 *Strathnaver*
Scene of savage nineteenth-century Sutherland clearances directed by the notorious Patrick Sellar.

70 *Steel?*
Disruption: schismatic event of 1843 when the Scottish Free Church was formed.

Alastair Mackie*

80 *Pieta*

This term was used by artists in the Middle Ages to describe Christ being wept over by his mother after the crucifixion. I think the poem was inspired by seeing TV pictures of Vietnamese women squatting on the ground, holding up their dead children. The poet offers no comfort.

81 *In Absentia*

A half-humorous poem on the modern religious debate on the question of the death of God, first announced by Nietzsche the German philosopher at the end of nineteenth century. The poet imagines one of the angels asking the question: why haven't we heard of God recently? Nobody seems to know. Baudelaire and Pascal, both religious thinkers, one a poet, the other a philosopher, fall into the emptiness of a universe without God, whom they believed in. Christ says 'It is finished'. Nietzsche laughs: his prophecy has come true. People keep going to church — occasionally. Finally God appears and says: Do what you like, I'm off.

82 *New Moon*

A series of different images of the new moon, after I saw it white in the cold sky of an April evening. It is a sickle; a Mongol shield; a laughing face; a white finger nail. And so on.

83 *Adolescence*

Based on an experience of my older daughter: she was crying one evening in her room and we couldn't get any word from her. The poet imagines he is his daughter. It is her voice that is speaking the poem. Adolescence is made up of: wanting to be left alone; unable to understand one's tears; feeling like a dumb beast; listening to the guitars in pop records etc. It begins in tears and ends in tears; she looks at her picture in the mirror.

84 *Mongol Quine*

An experience based on an incident while on holiday in a fishing village in the north of Scotland. A mongol child has a very low mental age and 'mongol' refers to the kind of Mongoloid features such children have. This girl was leaning over the harbour wall singing to herself, looking in the distance in the way these children do, as if they couldn't understand what is in front of them.

---

* These notes are provided by the poet himself.

84 *Mind on the Nichts*
A love poem addressed to my wife. 'Will you remember the nights
we made love' she says. 'Oh yes', I say; 'it's OK now when we're not
too old.' I try to be a bit critical. 'Later, it won't be easy. You'll grow
old, woman, you'll lose all your beauty. What then, when we're like
two old thin sticks in bed?' However, I end by saying, 'yes, I will
remember, my dear; I'll hold your thin aged hand. As I clasp it I'll
feel your blood move in it, very faint now, not as in the days when
we were young and made love. You'll be asleep, early.' A favourite
piece of mine.

86 *Scots Pegasus*
A humorous poem. Pegasus is the horse in Greek legend, which had
wings; it is a kind of symbol of poetic inspiration. The poet mounted
the horse and flew off into the sky. This Scottish horse however is a
poor, wooden, worm-eaten creature, who scarcely ever rises off the
ground. It is deliberately made comic. I suggest that other poets who
try to write in Scots never manage to succeed. The secret of getting
off the ground is to whisper the horseman's secret word into its ear. I
am really implying that *I* know the secret; other poets don't.

Burns Singer

97 *The Transparent Prisoner*
This was based on the actual experiences of a prisoner of war in the
1939–45 war. It tells of this man's condemnation to hacking coal for
sixteen hours a day. Singer met him when he, the prisoner of war,
had returned to Aberdeen University after the war to complete his
studies there.

101 *Sonnets for a Dying Man*
Of the sequence 'Sonnets for a Dying Man', in which father and son
or older and younger man (the present and the future) confront one
another, Singer said in a broadcast, 'In spite of all the vagaries of
modern life and philosophy I say that both life and death are
meaningful. I want, that is, to make an affirmation, an affirmation
and not an assertion, and I want to make it in the context of all our
knowledge and of all we merely think we know'. The manner of
these poems is, for me at least, that of a commentator, and they
require to be read slowly, expanded in the reader's thoughts and

related to the reader's past experience. [Note from Anne Cluysenaar's Introduction to *Selected Poems* 1977 (Carcanet Press)].

Stewart Conn

109 *Family Visit*
Kibble Palace: large ornate greenhouse in Glasgow Botanical Gardens.
Rijksmuseum: famous Amsterdam art gallery.

Douglas Dunn

122 *Witch-girl*
Gryfe, Deveron, Cree: three Scottish rivers.

Tom Leonard*

126 *The Good Thief*
I have heard people discuss this poem who did not seem to realise that it takes place at the time of the crucifixion. 'Paradise' was the name given by Celtic supporters to Parkhead, Glasgow Celtic's football ground.

127 *Paroakial*
A late-sixties' rebuke from a phoney internationalist. To explain all the electronic/drug jargon for younger readers would be to no purpose. If the language is dead, so be it.

128 *The Voyeur*
I interpret the character of the speaker as menacing and predatory, though overtly sugary. The addressed is not a woman, but a child. I'm trying to characterise a particular language usage in Scotland, a kind of cosy fireside-folkspeak that wraps up people's minds in safe comforting shibboleths like big knitted cardigans. Certain publications from Dundee are relevant, as are some awful homely Scottish television clergymen.

129 *Fireworks*
'The wee man' was the nickname given to Jimmy Johnstone, Celtic's outside-right. Bobby Lennox was a fast, high-scoring forward.
poastij stamp: a common metaphor for a shot which enters the goal through the top righthand corner as seen from the scorer's viewpoint.

* These notes are provided by the poet himself.

129 *Feed Ma Lamz*

A 'chanty rassler' is the contemptuous description applied to someone who has a high opinion of himself and of his ability to impress others, but who in fact talks, sells, or for example plays (if he is a footballer) in a manner that prompts one to consider the fruits of his labour as akin to the contents of a chamberpot, or chanty. The range of application is wide enough to include, if peripherally, 'one who bears false witness'.

G.B.H. — grievous bodily harm.

130 *Prisoner in thi Bar*

This is from a polemical sequence called *Ghostie Men*. The inclusion of this sequence in my collection *Intimate Voices 1965–83* no doubt contributed to the book's being banned in Scottish Central Region school libraries. I could not have asked for a clearer demonstration of the poem's argument.

130 *Four of the Belt*

This was written while the campaign to have the belt abolished in Strathclyde Region schools was in its final year, and one woman parent was taking the matter right to the European Court of Human Rights.

131 *A Priest Came on at Merkland Street*

The 116 lines here printed represent just over half of this asthmatic 'deliberately banal' monologue, taking place in the mind of a young man opposite and facing whom a priest has just sat down, in a coach on the Glasgow subway system. In the second half of the poem, the psychiatrist attempts a reply.

An early draft of the poem had as a kind of centrepiece a description of a coffin which can be seen on display in the Ancient Egyptian section of the Kelvingrove Museum, Glasgow. This small coffin lies half-open, revealing the skull and remains of what was once a priest called Nakht, who lived at a late period of the Twelfth Dynasty, which ended in 1778 BC. On the side of Nakht's coffin are painted two eyes: a descriptive card fixed to the glass viewcase notes that 'out of these the mummy was supposed to look'. The card also draws attention to the coffin lid: 'The lid has painted upon it a leopard skin, an emblem of the priesthood.'

I finally rejected this section of the poem as being too obviously 'symbolic', and too clear in its relation to the poem's last line:

brackets watch him he has a stoop and funny eyes.

Merkland Street: a station on the Glasgow Underground.

136 *Non Sum Qualis Eram*

The first two and last two lines are quotes from Ernest Dowson's 1896 poem of this title. The first eleven items on the list are alcoholic; the other three are drugs of the non-liquid variety.

Bibliography

Compiled by TOM HUBBARD
Librarian, Scottish Poetry Library

THE SCOTTISH POETRY LIBRARY

Anyone with a serious interest in Scottish poetry should not fail to take advantage of the services of this Library, which is based in Edinburgh's Royal Mile. The SPL is building a comprehensive collection of contemporary Scottish poetry in Gaelic, Scots and English; it also collects older Scottish poetry and, more selectively, poetry of other countries. Books, tapes and magazines are available for reference on the premises and for home borrowing, including by post. An information service on poetry and poets is in operation; special efforts are made to monitor the most recent developments in poetry all over Scotland. The Library's newsletter *Splash* is issued three times a year and contains lively reviews as well as news of readings, exhibitions and other poetry events around Scotland. For further details contact the Librarian, Scottish Poetry Library, Tweeddale Court, 14 High Street, Edinburgh EH1 1TE (Tel. 031-557 2876).

REFERENCE BOOKS

AITKEN, W. R. *Scottish Literature in English and Scots: A Guide to Information Sources*. Gale Research Company, 1982.
ROYLE, TREVOR *The Macmillan Companion to Scottish Literature*. Macmillan, 1983.
THOMSON, DERICK (ed.) *The Companion to Gaelic Scotland*. Blackwell, 1983.

GENERAL READING

THOMSON, DERICK *An Introduction to Gaelic poetry*. Gollancz, 1974.
LINDSAY, MAURICE *History of Scottish Literature*. Robert Hale, 1977.
Scottish Literature: A Study Guide. Prepared by William Donnelly, Sheila Hearn, and Glenda Norquay with Angus Calder. The Open University in Scotland, 1984.

WATSON, RODERICK *The Literature of Scotland*. Macmillan, 1984.

π: trimestrieel tijdschrift voor poezie / revue trimestrielle de poesie / poetry review, **3** (2) (1984). A magazine published by the European Association for the Promotion of Poetry. This particular issue carries a substantial feature on and of Scottish poetry; it includes articles on Scottish poetry in Gaelic, Scots and English by William Neill, Alan Bold and Trevor Royle.

ANTHOLOGIES

Four Points of a Saltire: The poetry of Sorley Maclean, George Campbell Hay, William Neill, Stuart MacGregor. Preface by Tom Scott. Reprographia, 1970.

KING, CHARLES (ed.) *Twelve Modern Scottish Poets*. Hodder and Stoughton, 1971.

LINDSAY, MAURICE (ed.) *Modern Scottish Poetry — An Anthology of the Scottish Renaissance*. Faber, 1966.

MACAULAY, DONALD (ed.) *Nua-bhàrdachd Ghàidhlig/ Modern Scottish Gaelic Poems by Sorley Maclean, George Campbell Hay, Derick Thomson, Iain Crichton Smith and Donald MacAulay: A Bilingual Anthology*. Southside, 1976.

MURRAY, BRIAN & SMYTH, SYDNEY (eds) *A Sense of Belonging: Six Scottish Poets of the Seventies*. Blackie, 1977. The poets are Stewart Conn, Douglas Dunn, Tom Leonard, Liz Lochhead, William McIlvanney and Edwin Morgan.

MACKIE, ALASTAIR, TAIT, WILLIAM & McDONALD, ELLIE. *Twa Chiels and a Lass, Reading Their Own Poems*. Scotsoun, 1979. Cassette audio tape.

SCOTT, ALEXANDER (ed.) *Modern Scots Verse 1922–1977*. Akros, 1978.

PERIODICALS

The value of the literary magazines cannot be overestimated: they are essential for readers wishing to keep in touch with the latest Scottish poetry. Check that your school, college, university or public library stocks a good selection of these publications; they depend on subscriptions for their very survival. Further information on the magazines is available from the Scottish Poetry Library, which also has current issues on sale.

Akros (three times a year) 1965–83

Aynd (bi-monthly) 1983–

Blind Serpent (irregular) 1984–

Books in Scotland (irregular) 1978–

Cencrastus (quarterly) 1979–

Chapman (three times a year) 1970–

Clanjamfrie (occasional) 1984–

Edinburgh Review (quarterly) 1984–. Successor to the *New Edinburgh Review*.

The Gairfish (occasional) 1983–

Gairm (quarterly) 1952–. Devoted to writing in Gaelic.

The Glasgow Magazine (twice a year) 1982–

Graffiti (twice a year) 1980–

Lallans: the magazine for writing in Lowland Scots (twice a year) 1973–

Lines Review (quarterly) 1952–

New Edinburgh Review (monthly, later quarterly) 1969–84. Succeeded by the *Edinburgh Review*.

New Writing Scotland (once a year) 1983–

Radical Scotland (bi-monthly) relaunched 1983–. Usually carries a poetry page.

Scotia Rampant (occasional) 1985–

Scotia Review (three times a year) 1972–78

Scottish International (quarterly, later monthly) 1968–74

Scottish Literary Journal (twice a year) 1974–

Scottish Poetry (once a year) 1966–76

Scottish Review (quarterly) 1975–85. A relaunch in 1986 has been announced.

Splash: Newsletter of the Scottish Poetry Library Association (three times a year) 1984–. Since issue No. 4, this publication has been carrying short reviews of new or neglected Scottish poetry.

Studies in Scottish literature (quarterly, now annual) 1963–

Verse (twice a year) 1984–

Weighbauk (occasional) 1974–

Words (three times a year) 1976–81

THE TWELVE POETS

In citing articles on these poets, I have concentrated on items which discuss either a poet's collected work to date, or a particular poem included in the present anthology. I exclude reviews except where they assess a complete or near complete collection of a poet's work to date. My one exception to this rule concerns our youngest poet, Valerie Gillies: here I have cited reviews of her most recent book.

G. S. Fraser

Poems of G. S. Fraser. Ed. by Ian Fletcher and John Lucas. Leicester University Press, 1981.

A Stranger and Afraid: The Autobiography of an Intellectual. Carcanet New Press, 1983.

PICK, J. B. *Poems of G. S. Fraser. Lines Review,* **79** (December 1981), pp. 8–11.

BRUCE, GEORGE *Poems of G. S. Fraser. Akros,* **51** (October 1983), pp. 79–84.

SCOTT, PATRICK G. S. Fraser. *Cencrastus,* **16** (Spring 1984), pp. 31–3.

BRACKENBURY, ROSALIND Remembering George Fraser. *Chapman,* **40** (Spring 1985), pp. 61–5.

George Campbell Hay *also known as* Deòrsa Caimbeul Hay or Deòrsa MacIain Deòrsa

Fuaran Sleibh. William Maclellan, 1947.

Wind on Loch Fyne. Oliver and Boyd, 1948.

O na ceithir airdean. Oliver and Boyd, 1952.

Mochtàr is Dùghall. Department of Celtic, University of Glasgow, 1982.

NEILL, WILLIAM The poetry of George Campbell Hay. *Scotia Review,* **8** (December 1974), pp. 50–6.

MARTIN, ANGUS *Kintyre: The Hidden Past.* John Donald, 1984, pp. 48–71. Chapter 3 is devoted to 'George Campbell Hay: bard of Kintyre'.

BURNS, JOHN George Campbell Hay. *Radical Scotland,* **9** (June/July 1984), p. 25.

BURNS, JOHN Generous spirited heart: the poetry of George Campbell Hay. *Cencrastus,* **18** (Autumn 1984), pp. 28–30.

MEEK, DONALD E. Land and loyalty: the Gaelic verse of George Campbell Hay. *Chapman,* **39** (Autumn 1984), pp. 2–8.

THOMSON, DERICK George Campbell Hay: a tribute. *Scottish Review,* **35** (August 1984), pp. 42–4.

SMITH, IAIN CRICHTON George Campbell Hay: language at large. *Scottish Review,* **35** (August 1984), pp. 45–50.

RANKIN, ROBERT A. George Campbell Hay as I knew him. *Chapman,* **40** (Spring 1985), pp. 1–12.

NEILL, WILLIAM George Campbell Hay (1915–84). *Lallans,* **25** (Martinmas 1985), pp. 33–6. In Scots.

Maurice Lindsay

Collected Poems. Paul Harris, 1979.
A Net to Catch the Winds, and Other Poems. Robert Hale, 1981.
Thank You For Having Me: A Personal Memoir. Robert Hale, 1983.
The French Mosquitoes' Woman, and Other Diversions and Poems. Robert Hale, 1985.

> CAMPBELL, DONALD A different way of being right: the poetry of Maurice Lindsay. *Akros*, **24** (April 1974), pp. 22–6.
>
> LINDSAY, MAURICE I belong to Glasgow. In: LINDSAY, MAURICE (ed.) *As I Remember: Ten Scottish Authors Recall How Writing Began For Them.* Robert Hale, 1979, pp. 59–77.
>
> MACINTYRE, LORN M. The poetry of Maurice Lindsay. *Akros*, **42** (December 1979), pp. 44–53.

W. S. Graham

Collected Poems 1942–1977. Faber, 1979.

> DUXBURY, ROBERT The poetry of W. S. Graham. *Akros*, **38** (August 1978), pp. 62–71.
>
> REID, ALASTAIR Signature of all things. *Lines Review*, **75** (December 1980), pp. 5–7.
>
> MORGAN, EDWIN The poetry of W. S. Graham. *Cencrastus*, **5** (Summer 1981), pp. 8–10.

Derick Thomson *also known as* Ruaraidh MacThòmais

Creachadh na clàrsaich / Plundering the Harp: Collected Poems 1940–1980. Macdonald, 1982.
Why Gaelic Matters. Saltire Society/An Comunn Gaidhealach, 1984.

> THOMSON, DERICK A man reared in Lewis. In: LINDSAY, MAURICE (ed.) *As I Remember: Ten Scottish Authors Recall How Writing Began For Them.* Robert Hale, 1979, pp. 123–40.
>
> DHEÒRSA, MACIAIN *Creachadh na clarsaich. Gairm*, **122** (An t-earrach 1983), pp. 183–6. In Gaelic.
>
> CAMPBELL, MILES Origin and exile. *Cencrastus*, **13** (Summer 1983), p. 46.
>
> THOMPSON, FRANK Plundering the harp. *Books in Scotland*, **13** (Autumn 1983), pp. 19–20.
>
> SMITH, IAIN CRICHTON Derek [*sic*] Thomson's 'Clann nighean an sgadain'. *Akros*, **51** (October 1983), pp. 42–4.

WHYTE, CHRISTOPHER Derick Thomson: reluctant symbolist. *Chapman*, **38** (Spring 1984), pp. 1–6.

SMITH, IAIN CRICHTON The poetry of Derick Thomson. *Scottish Review*, **37** (February/May 1985), pp. 24–30.

MACFHIONNLAIGH, FEARGHAS Borbhan comair: ath-sgrùdadh air bàrdachd Ruaraidh MhicThòmais. *Gairm*, **124** (An samhradh 1985), pp. 259–71. In Gaelic.

Alastair Mackie

Soundings. Akros, 1966.

Clytach. Akros, 1972.

At the Heich Kirk-yaird: A Hielant Sequence. Akros, 1974.

Back-green Odyssey, and Other Poems. Rainbow Books, 1980.

GARIOCH, ROBERT Alastair Mackie's poetry. *Lallans*, **1** (Mairtinmas 1973), pp. 10–2. In Scots.

MASON, LEONARD Two north-east makars: Alexander Scott and Alastair Mackie. A study of their Scots poetry. *Akros*, 1975.

BRUCE, GEORGE The poetry of Alastair Mackie, or Feet on the grun. *Akros*, **33** (April 1977), pp. 76–86.

GILLIES, MARGARET Alastair Mackie's 'Pieta'. *Akros*, **51** (October 1983), pp. 45–7.

Burns Singer

Still and All. Secker and Warburg, 1957.

Living Silver: An Impression of the British Fishing Industry. [prose] Secker and Warburg, 1957.

Collected Poems. Ed. by W. A. S. Keir. Preface by Hugh MacDiarmid. Secker and Warburg, 1970.

Selected Poems. Ed. by Anne Cluysenaar. Carcanet New Press, 1977.

MACDIARMID, HUGH *The Company I've Kept*. Hutchinson, 1966, pp. 217–8.

SCHMIDT, MICHAEL Burns Singer. *Poetry Nation*, **5** (1975), pp. 94–9.

Stewart Conn

Thunder in the Air. Akros, 1967.

The Chinese Tower. Macdonald, 1967.

Stoats in the Sunlight. Hutchinson, 1968.

The King. [play] In: *New English Dramatists*, **14**. Penguin, 1970, pp. 157–83.

An Ear to the Ground. Hutchinson, 1972.

The Burning: A Play. Calder and Boyars, 1973.

The Aquarium; The Man in the Green Muffler; I Didn't Always Live Here. [plays] John Calder, 1976.

Under the Ice. Hutchinson, 1978.

Thistlewood. [play] Woodhouse Books, 1979.

In the Kibble Palace — Poems, New and Selected. Bloodaxe Books (in press).

BRUCE, GEORGE 'Bound by necessity': the poetry of Stewart Conn. *Akros*, **40** (April 1979), pp. 58–70.

SMITH, IAIN CRICHTON Towards the human: the poetry of Stewart Conn. *New Edinburgh Review*, **62** (Summer 1983), pp. 20–2.

SCOTT, ALEXANDER Stewart Conn's 'Todd'. *Akros*, **51** (October 1983), pp. 52–3.

CONN, STEWART Introduction to selected poems. In: ABSE, DANNIE (ed.) *Modern Poets in Focus 3.* Corgi Books, 1971.

AITCHISON, JAMES The poetry of Stewart Conn. *Glasgow Review*, **iv** (January/March 1973), pp. 13–14.

CONN, STEWART A tale of two cities: a poet in Glasgow and Edinburgh. *Scottish Review*, **18** (May 1980), pp. 3–8.

Douglas Dunn

Terry Street. Faber, 1969.

Backwaters. The Review, 1971.

The Happier life. Faber, 1972.

Love or Nothing. Faber, 1974.

Barbarians. Faber, 1979.

St Kilda's Parliament. Faber, 1981.

Europa's Lover. Bloodaxe Books, 1982.

Elegies. Faber, 1985.

Secret Villages. [short stories] Faber, 1985.

DUXBURY, ROBERT The poetry of Douglas Dunn. *Akros*, **14** (August 1979), pp. 47–61.

DUNN, DOUGLAS Exile and unexile. *Cencrastus*, **16** (Spring 1984), pp. 4–6.

Tom Leonard

My Name is Tom. [sound-poem score] Good Elf, 1978.

If Only Bunty Was Here: A Drama Sequence of Totally Undramatic Non-sequiturs. Print Studio Press, 1979.

Intimate Voices: Selected Work 1965–1983. Galloping Dog Press, 1984.
Satires and Profanities. [prose pieces] STUC, 1985.

> McGRATH, TOM Tom Leonard: man with two heads. *Akros,* **24** (April 1974), pp. 40–9.

> MULRINE, STEPHEN Tom Leonard's 'The good thief'. *Akros,* **51** (October 1983), pp. 54–5.

> HAMILTON, ROBIN The speak of the city. *New Edinburgh Review,* **65** (Spring 1984), pp. 39–40.

> KIRKWOOD, COLIN Vulgar eloquence: Tom Leonard's *Intimate Voices, 1965–1983. Cencrastus,* **20** (Spring 1985), pp. 21–3.

Liz Lochhead

Dreaming Frankenstein and Collected Poems. Polygon, 1984.
True Confessions and New Clichés. Polygon, 1985.

> LOCHHEAD, LIZ A Protestant girlhood. In: ROYLE, TREVOR (ed.) *Jock Tamson's ·Bairns: Essays on a Scots Childhood.* Hamish Hamilton, 1977, pp. 112–25.

> ROYLE, TREVOR *Dreaming Frankenstein and collected Poems. Books in Scotland,* **16** (Autumn 1984), p. 16.

> FURNISS-SANDER, KRISTINE *Dreaming Frankenstein and Collected Poems. Radical Scotland,* **10** (August/September 1984), p. 28.

> RELICH, MARIO *Dreaming Frankenstein and Collected Poems. Lines Review,* **91** (December 1984), pp. 40–2.

> RIACH, ALAN A growing end for Scottish verse? *Chapman,* **40** (Spring 1985), pp. 75–6.

Valerie Gillies

Each Bright Eye: Selected Poems 1971–1976. Canongate, 1977.
Bed of Stone. Canongate, 1984.
(Ed.) *School of Poets Calendar 1986.* [calendar anthology of work by other poets] School of Poets, 1985.

> DUNN, DOUGLAS *Bed of Stone* [etc.]. *Books in Scotland,* **16** (Autumn 1984), pp. 16–17.

> STEPHEN, IAN Valerie Gillies: *Bed of Stone. Chapman,* **39** (Autumn 1984), pp. 64–5.

> NEILL, WILLIAM *Bed of Stone. Lines Review,* **92** (March 1985), pp. 40–3.